Praise for *The Untold S*

Entertaining, fascinating, deeply researched, and cr... *Books* is full of surprises. I worked in publishing for thirty years and was amazed how much I learned about the industry. No other book provides such a comprehensive and witty overview. *The Untold Story of Books* is a must-read for authors, aspiring authors, and anyone who loves books. The publishing industry is often shrouded in mystery. This book lifts the veil and provides a fresh, new, compelling perspective.

—Mark Chimsky, former editorial director of Harper San Francisco, former director of trade paperbacks at Little Brown, and former editor-in-chief of the trade paperback division at Macmillan

Castleman has created a unique, highly readable title... It's delightful the way he relates the history of the technological innovations that have propelled book publishing. One of my favorite elements is the way he explains the economics of publishing from a writer's point of view. I'll be telling many people about *The Untold Story of Books*. It's a tremendous contribution.

—Laura Lent, former chief of collections at San Francisco Public Library

Quirky, comprehensive, opinionated, and massively entertaining, *The Untold Story of Books* combines Castleman's fifty years of bittersweet experience as an author with his vivid, amusing history of book publishing. Castleman beautifully conveys the essence of writing—of creating—today.

—Daniel Ben-Horin, author of *Substantial Justice*

The Untold Story is excellent: fun, amazingly comprehensive, surprisingly informative, and often amusing. A great read.

—Jeffrey Klein, author of *The Black Hole Affair*, and former editor-in-chief of *Mother Jones* magazine

The Untold Story of Books is full of fascinating and entertaining history, most of which was new to me, plus a comprehensive and realistic (if sometimes discouraging) picture of what is happening in book publishing today. Past and present—all informative and enjoyable!

—Gillian Roberts, author of the *Amanda Pepper* mysteries

The Untold Story of Books is a real page-turner. I loved Castleman's analysis of book sales in terms of units sold and the money authors earn. And I loved the hilarious anecdotes about book piracy, publisher mergers, and other elements of the book business. As soon as I finished *The Untold Story of Books*, I started recommending it to writer friends.

—Chris Carlsson, former bookseller and author of *Hidden San Francisco: A Guide to Lost Landscapes, Unsung Heroes and Radical Histories*, and *When Shells Crumble*

Fascinating, incredibly informative, and humorous, a must read for every writer. Castleman *knows* the book business like no other author—and explains it to the rest of us. I came away with a new understanding of publishing, the present state of the industry, and the gritty realities that writers have always faced—and still do... Castleman's writing is riveting! While *The Untold Story* dissolves delusions of grandeur for most authors, Castleman helps us accept without shame the reality that we should keep our day jobs knowing we're writing and publishing for the pleasure of the process—and for any readers who discover and enjoy our books.

—Jane Sloven, author of the novel *Termination of Benefits* and *Compassionate Journey: Honoring Our Mothers' Stories*

Castleman is frank, personable, and likable. He conveys his experiences as an author directly and convincingly, without sounding either preachy or aggrieved.

—Larry Gonick, author of *The Cartoon History of the Universe*

Authors everywhere believe that if they just write well enough, or have the right agent, or burn incense while writing, they can produce bestsellers. *The Untold Story of Books* splashes cold water on their faces, while presenting refreshing, important, much-needed perspectives on the evolution of present- day publishing.

—Laura Fraser, author of *An Italian Affair*

I loved—and hated—*The Untold Story of Books*. Loved it for its wonderful insights. Castleman celebrates books' historic journey as humankind's most beloved form of documentation. But hated it because he shows how in every era, most authors have been schmucks who let others control publishing and deny them the financial fruits of their labors.

—Josie Brown, author of *The Housewife Assassin's Handbook* series

Every author, every aspiring author, and everyone who cares deeply about books and reading should read *The Untold Story of Books*. It's deeply researched yet a fast, fun read. It takes a serious look at a serious subject, yet it's remarkably amusing.

—David Steinberg, author of *Erotic by Nature: A Celebration of Life, of Love, and Our Wonderful Bodies*

The Untold Story of Books combines a fascinating history of publishing with Castleman's personal tale of fifty years as an author. I loved Castleman's honesty about his writing income, and his prognostications about the likely future of publishing. I especially enjoyed his explanation of the origin of the term "blurb."

—John Boe, Ph.D., author of *Living the Shakespearean Life*

Reading *The Untold Story of Books* was like having my ear pressed against forbidden walls. It's super informative about how the bittersweet book business evolved and packed with straightforward tips on navigating its stormy waters. This book is a must-read for everyone who loves books and all those interested in writing them.

—Virginia London, editor and creative writing teacher

Whether you're a reader or a published or aspiring writer, you'll love this witty guide to the mysterious, important, aggravating, and endlessly surprising business of publishing.

—**Marty Klein, Ph.D., author of** *His Porn, Her Pain: Confronting America's Porn Panic with Honest Talk About Sex*

This book should be required reading for anyone with the pluck to undertake book writing today. It's lucid, witty, comprehensive, and sometimes frightening. I wish I'd had the benefit of Castleman's analysis years ago.

—**Frank Viviano, author of** *Blood Washes Blood*

The Untold Story of Books is compelling and beautifully written. Castleman does a masterful job conveying how publishing evolved from Gutenberg to today. Authors both published and aspiring will definitely benefit from his keen insights into the industry, but all book lovers will gain a deeper understanding of the book business, and what they need to do to keep books and reading thriving.

—**Marc Mauer, author of** *The Race to Incarcerate*

Castleman opened my eyes to the crapshoot that writing books and publishing and selling them has always been.

—**Ron Lichty, co-author of** *Managing the Unmanageable: Rules, Tools, and Insights for Managing Software People and Teams*

I'm a first-time author, therefore confused. I learned so much from *The Untold Story of Books*! Castleman's delightful, insightful history of publishing provides great perspective. Completing the book, I felt liberated, like I'd just been untied from playing Isaac on Abraham's altar.

—**Eugene Larkin, author of** *Seeking Soteria*

The Untold Story of Books is actually multiple untold stories about publishing, each more informative and entertaining than the last. Castleman's concept of the three publishing businesses is brilliant, and serves as a very helpful frame to understand the past, present, and future of the industry. I recommend it to every author, aspiring author, and book lover.

—**Bernard Ohanian, author of** *Baseball in America* **and** *A Day in the Life of Italy*

The Untold Story of Books is fantastic. Castleman is a fine researcher who writes with crystal clarity... I can't imagine a better analysis of today's book business.

—**Jeffrey James Higgins, author of** *Unseen Evil Lurks Among Us* **and** *Furious: Sailing Into Terror*

Absolutely essential for both veteran and aspiring authors, *The Untold Story of Books* is a goldmine of publishing history and current trends in the complex, often inscrutable world of books. Highly recommended!

—**Jean Burgess, Ph.D., author of** *Collaborative Stage Directing: A Guide to Creating and Managing a Positive Theatre Environment*

The Untold Story of Books is a compelling read that illuminates the confusing quagmire of the book industry from its earliest beginnings until the present day. Castleman's meticulous research, fast pace and good-humored voice kept me completely absorbed. Now that I understand how the business of books has treated authors for centuries, I have a context for my own bumpy experiences and a slew of tools for future decision-making.

—Nicola Ranson, author of *A Slice of Orange* and *Plant Talk: When the Tree Hugs You Back*

Castleman's tone is very friendly. His research is impressive. I learned a great deal I didn't know... the origins of publishing terms—pulp fiction, copyright, upper/lower case—and the long, sad history of book piracy, which is especially fascinating since we see so many complaints about piracy today. I also appreciated Castleman's perspective on self-publishing vs. the misnomer called "traditional" publishing. Every writer should read this book. Anyone who loves books should also find it fascinating and entertaining.

—Ann Buscho, Ph.D., author of *The Parent's Guide to Birdnesting: A Child-Centered Solution to Co-Parenting During Separation or Divorce*

The Untold Story of Books is quite valuable to anyone interested in books. Very eye-opening, especially about the long sad history of book piracy, and the grim realities of publishing today. I learned a lot. I imagine every writer would.

—Martha Miller, author of *Me Inside*

The Untold Story of Books is a clear, forceful account of publishing that writers and many others should enjoy. The biggest revelation for me: what we consider "traditional" or "conventional" publishing was simply an 80-year aberration over six centuries when almost all authors self-published.

—Laird Harrison, author of *Fallen Lake*

If only I could have read *The Untold Story of Books* before writing mine. It provides invaluable insights into the often-confusing, often-frustrating, sometimes-infuriating business of books. And if you're a book lover, *The Untold Story of Books* tells the fascinating, entertaining story of how book publishing evolved into what it is today. Two thumbs up!

—Robin Wolaner, author of *Naked in the Boardroom*

The Untold Story of Books is a stunning exploration of the history of book writing, printing, publishing, and reading from ancient times to the present day. It gives authors centuries of context for the challenges they face in today's Digital Age. And it provides book lovers with new understanding that the books they read are the product of a tortuous journey through the evolution of printing. I recommend it to authors, readers, publishers, and everyone who loves books.

—Chris Dickon, author of *The Foreign Burial of American War Dead and Dutch Children of African American Liberator.*

The Untold Story of Books presents a realistic and comprehensive picture of publishing today. I had never heard anyone divide publishing into three separate book businesses as Castleman has. That was quite illuminating. I wish I'd had the benefit of this book *before* I began writing mine. I commend Castleman for having the courage to write this book.

—Ellen Mason, author of *No Space for Love*

The Untold Story of Books is outstanding! Exhaustively researched and vital for all authors, Castleman's history of the industry and his tales of his own travails are fascinating. What a valuable resource! *The Untold Story of Books* is a stark reminder of the many challenges of publishing.

—Deborah Gray, author of *How to Import Wine: An Insider's Guide*

Castleman's explanations of the economics driving the industry are eye-opening and often amusing. A wonderful book, and a great gift for every author, aspiring author, and book lover you know.

—David Fenton, author of *The Activist's Media Handbook: Lessons from Fifty Years as a Progressive Agitator*

The Untold Story of Books so captured my attention that I read every word. I appreciated Castleman's straight-forward analysis of the publishing industry's checkered history from Gutenberg to today. *The Untold Story* is both discouraging AND encouraging. The bad news: More than 7,000 books are released every day with most selling fewer than 100 copies. The good: Millions of authors are still writing good books, and many millions of book lovers are still reading them.

—Susan Meller, author of *Labels of Empire*

The Untold Story of Books takes us through centuries of epic changes in the world of books and publishing, and explains publishing today better than anything else I've read. It reflects Castleman's tremendous amount of research. His book has helped me understand why book publishing today is so frustratingly different from what I encountered when I published my first trade book in 1990.

—Diane Dreher, author of *The Tao of Inner Peace*

Michael Castleman's *The Untold Story of Books* is a bible for writers. This uniquely informative publishing history balances the bad news with—yes!—some good. An indispensable toolkit for authors as they navigate publishing today.

—Sarah McGinty, author of *Power Talk*

I didn't realize how badly I needed *The Untold Story of Books* until I read it. Castleman's seminal work provides valuable insights into the evolution of publishing for anyone involved in today's brave new world of books—readers, writers, booksellers, publishers, agents, and editors. If you're involved in books as a reader or writer, read this one!

—DeAnne Musolf, co-author (with Eric Heiden M.D. and Massimo Testa M.D.) of *Faster, Better, Stronger: 10 Proven Secrets to a Healthier Body*

The Untold Story of Books is comprehensive and intriguing. Castleman documents how words have been copied without permission since Gutenberg, as well as why publishers are transferring more responsibility to today's authors—but less money. Only after reading Castleman did I understand why I had such different experiences between my first book and my most recent.

—**Jo Freeman, author of** ***We Will Be Heard: Women's Struggles for Political Power in the United States***

Impeccably researched and engagingly written, *The Untold Story of Books is*] filled with invaluable advice and perspective for authors and aspiring authors alike. Best of all, it offers reassurance that this alluring business has always been tough on most writers.

—**Dawn McIntyre, author of** ***The Paper Pirate***

For almost 50 years I've been writing books and witnessing changes, shifts, and upsets in the world of publishing. I had no idea why everything kept changing—for writers and publishers alike. Then I read Michael Castleman's *The Untold Story of Books*. Brilliantly researched and engagingly written, it traces the long arc of book publishing from Gutenberg to Amazon and spells out how the industry evolved and what it all means. Whether you're a grizzled publishing vet or a fresh-faced newbie drawn to long-form writing, Castleman's fine book provides insight into the world of publishing, the world we love.

—**Robert Aquinas McNally, author of** ***The Modoc War*** **and the forthcoming** ***Cast out of Eden: The Untold Story of John Muir, Indigenous Peoples, and the American Wilderness***

Michael Castleman has compiled a uniquely valuable, well-written examination of book publishing and what it means for authors. *The Untold Story of Books* is filled with history, insight, and even hope. If you love books, it's definitely worth reading.

—**Betty Bolté, author of** ***Hometown Heroines: True Stories of Bravery, Daring, and Adventure***

The
Untold
Story
of Books

A Writer's History
of Book Publishing

Michael Castleman

THE UNNAMED PRESS
LOS ANGELES, CA

AN UNNAMED PRESS BOOK

Copyright © 2024 by Michael Castleman

All rights reserved, including the right to reproduce this book or portions thereof in any form whatsoever. Permissions inquiries may be directed to info@unnamedpress.com

Published in North America by the Unnamed Press.

www.unnamedpress.com

Unnamed Press, and the colophon, are registered trademarks of Unnamed Media LLC.

Paperback ISBN: 978-1-961884-08-3
EBook ISBN: 978-1-961884-09-0
LCCN: 2023947200

Cover design and typeset by Jaya Nicely

Manufactured in the United States of America

Distributed by Publishers Group West

First Edition

Dedicated to my parents, Mim and Lou Castleman, who once asked,
"A *writer*? How on earth will you make a living?"

And to Anne Simons,
for more than fifty years my partner in love and life,
who always encouraged me to chase my dreams
and never once said, "Mike, get a job."

It is striking how frequently people will comment that the book business is just not what it used to be. With great regularity, members of the industry wistfully hearken back to a golden age when individuals entered this line of work because they cared about books, not money; when publishers engaged with writers, not bestseller lists; and when the American public supported the neighborhood bookseller, who worked so hard to make a living. However, if one actually tries to locate this bygone era, it keeps receding further and further into the past. The years that present-day book people look back on so fondly were not seen as particularly golden by those living through them.

—Laura J. Miller, *Reluctant Capitalists: Bookselling and the Culture of Consumption*

CONTENTS

The
Untold
Story
of Books

= Introduction =

Two old jokes crystalize the book business:

•How do you make a small fortune in publishing? *Start with a large one.*

•What's the difference between an author and an extra-large pizza? *An extra-large pizza can feed a family.*

Of course, I'm not the first to address the bittersweetness of publishing and book writing, or the fact that very few authors—or publishers, agents, or booksellers—become Shakespeare or get rich. Everyone who dips a toe into the roiling waters of publishing quickly learns that the book business is no beach party.

Which raises a question: Why do authors and book people get up every morning obsessed with writing and books? As one would expect, reasons vary, but based on forty-five years as an author, ten years as an editor, and innumerable interactions with people involved in every aspect of publishing, one reason stands head and shoulders above all others. Book people *love* books.

We love to hold them, turn their pages, read and collect them, learn from them, thrill to their artistry, and marvel at their ability to transport us to distant times and places and insert us into the lives of people very different from ourselves. Then, when we've reached "The End," we love to ponder books' meanings and discuss them with anyone up for the conversation.

To me, books are the bricks that form the foundation of culture. All the book people I've ever known have felt proud to count themselves among the culture's bricklayers. They've all felt passionate about contributing to humanity's ever-unfolding saga.

Forty-Four Years of Research

Since 1980, I've published nineteen books, one almost every other year: fourteen nonfiction titles dealing with health and sexuality, four mystery novels, and this history. From the moment I signed my first contract, I've researched the industry, figuring that studying its business side might aid my career. When I attended writing conferences, instead of attending the how-to-get-published panels or standing in signing lines for A-list authors, I was among the few quizzing the publishers: *How do you determine print runs? Why don't you advertise more?* Publishers always expressed surprise: *You're interested in the business side?* Few authors they dealt with were, unless it had to do with their royalties.

Turns out, you can understand your royalties a lot better if you understand the industry. For four decades, I've followed the book business avidly (see Sources and Bibliography). I devoured every publishing book I could find, among them many memoirs, notably *At Random* (1977), the reminiscences of Bennett Cerf (1898–1971), founder of Random House. He depicted the industry as a delightfully gossipy enterprise fueled by cocktail parties and weekends in the Hamptons. *At Random* was entertaining, but not particularly informative.

Then I read *Book Business: Publishing Past, Present, and Future* (2001), by Jason Epstein, Random House's longtime editorial director. In contrast to his boss, he focused not on personalities and martinis, but on the economic history of publishing from World War II to the millennium. I loved it—and figured that if Epstein's six-decade perspective could produce such fascinating insights, perhaps an investigation of publishing's entire six-hundred-year sweep might provide even more.

That is the mission of *The Untold Story of Books*, to provide authors and book lovers with informed perspective on an industry often shrouded in mystery and mythology. This book is my attempt to lift the veil, to demonstrate how the book business actually developed and continues to evolve today. Ultimately, I hope it provides writers with a better understanding of their industry, especially the new possibilities and perils of the third book business.

Three Book Businesses

Book publishing has experienced three distinct epochs with three different economic strategies ("business models"). I call them the first, second, and third book businesses. Each involved technological revolutions in printing that allowed fewer individuals (and later publishing houses) to produce more copies of more books faster and cheaper per copy ("unit cost"). Each book business developed its own unique economics and center of gravity, and its own paths to success despite daunting challenges. And in each, what most influenced the bottom line was neither the writers nor publishers, but the way ever-increasing numbers of readers responded to the evolving industry.

The first book business began with Johannes Gutenberg's invention of movable type and lasted 450 years through the end of the nineteenth century. It was an author-centric cottage industry, "author-centric" because entrepreneurial writers formed its core. Publishers, as we know them, did not exist. In a world without publishers, most authors were entrepreneurs who hired printers, paid to publish, and marketed their books on their own.

The printers those authors hired walked a greased tightrope. Printing books was risky. Presses, paper, and ink were expensive, and books cost more than most readers could afford. Many book printers went bankrupt, including Gutenberg. Of course, every business involves considerable risk. But few people outside publishing appreciate how challenging it is to find what readers want and deliver it to them.

During the late nineteenth century, publishing industrialized, and literacy grew. Over several decades, Gutenberg-style hand-operated presses yielded to huge steam-driven machines that could print thousands of books in the blink of an eye. Industrialized printing produced substantial reductions in unit cost, which allowed more people to buy more books, read them, and dream of writing them.

By World War I, industrial publishing produced the second book business, now called "traditional publishing," though it lasted only eighty of the book business's six hundred years. The new model was publisher-centric. As it developed, authors stopped hiring printers. Instead, the new publishers contracted with authors and gave many of them money up front, advances—actually loans—to write manuscripts, which the publishers printed and marketed. This change relieved authors of entrepreneurial headaches. But as the second book business matured, publishers gained firm control over the new model, and many authors felt they had become cogs in a vast machine.

The second book business made some publishers and a tiny fraction of authors richer than anyone had previously thought possible. But the book business remained daunting. While unit costs fell, publishers' overall cost of doing business increased substantially. Printing and distributing more copies of many more titles strained publishers' resources. Many couldn't hack it. They either went bankrupt or merged with other houses.

Mention "merger," and the term conjures visions of equal partners combining forces for mutual benefit. Actually, *absorbed* was more like it. Shortly before bankruptcy, in fire sales, failing publishers relinquished to stronger houses their two assets: their names and backlists. They became "imprints," wholly owned subsidiaries. They continued to release books but were no longer living, breathing enterprises. From 1970 through the millennium, publishing witnessed more than three hundred mergers. During that period, the number of "major" publishers, the New York houses with familiar names, decreased from several dozen to just five, the Big Five.

Around the millennium, the digital revolution launched the third book business. Computer technology—digital book design, desktop publishing, e-books, and print-on-demand—powered a streamlined model that once again dramatically reduced books' unit cost. Readers' habits changed too, as access to books diversified and personal entertainment choices increased. In the third book business, publishers are still very much with us, but publishing has become increasingly sales-and-distribution-centric, dominated by Amazon.

The first and second book businesses were manufacturing enterprises. Book manufacture was costly, but a sufficient proportion of most publishers' titles sold well enough to keep the lights on. The third book business has upended that. In the digital age, producing books has become the easy part. Using Sqribble software, authors can turn manuscripts into e-books in an hour for less than $100. And if you want print copies, say two hundred, with print-on-demand, they can be yours in a week or two, with each copy costing no more than a latte. Consequently, releases have exploded. During the entire twentieth century, the second book business published approximately 2.5 million titles. Today, publishers and self-publishers produce that many new releases *every year or two*. The avalanche of new titles has changed the very definition of "publishing" and how readers find, enjoy, and react to books.

Today's unprecedented book glut has pushed median sales off a cliff. Some titles—around one in thirteen thousand—still sell zillions. But nowadays, only 6 percent of new releases sell one thousand copies, and four out of five self-published titles sell fewer than one hundred. Books published by the Big Five are best positioned to succeed, but it's by no means rare for their titles to sell only a few hundred copies.

As the first book business evolved into the second, publishing's center of gravity shifted from authors to publishers. As the second has evolved into the third, the fulcrum has moved from publishers toward Amazon.

Since its founding in 1994, Amazon has bankrupted many publishers, three-quarters of independent booksellers, and several bookstore chains. Since 2015, independent booksellers and publishers have bounced back. Still, as I write, Amazon accounts for 40 percent of trade sales. ("Trade" means books sold in bookstores, not textbooks or business, religious, or technical titles.) Amazon's huge market share means it can demand wholesale discounts that squeeze publishers.

The third book business has produced amazing new opportunities for success. *Fifty Shades of Grey*, which first appeared as an e-book in 2011, has sold 150 million copies. But like its two predecessors, the third book business presents existential challenges daily. Keep that in mind the next time a publisher offers you a no-advance contract, like the one I signed for this book.

What does the third book business portend for authors and those who aspire to see their names on book covers? The current model has granted authors one magnificent benefit: easy, affordable self-publishing. But that gift comes with a crushing impediment: in the United States alone, there are 7,400 new releases every day, more than *five every minute*. Meanwhile, most new releases sell in two figures—rarely beyond authors' friends and families. Want to learn how few friends you have? Self-publish a book. Of course, some authors write expressly for their family and friends, without commercial aspirations. But the vast majority of authors I've known have craved a mass audience and have struggled to understand why it's so elusive.

Perspective

My book-writing career has spanned the decades from the second book business into the third. The transition has not been kind to most authors. Authors Guild surveys show that since 2009, members' median book-related income has fallen by *half*.

Still, I love to write. I reveled in it before I made a dime as a writer. I was the weird kid who thought term papers were the best part of school. In college, I won a writing prize and decided to write for a living. I struggled for a dozen years until I hit my stride. In the 1980s and '90s, I made good money from magazine writing (during the heyday of that industry) and from books. Two of my titles produced enviable royalties. But like many writers of my generation, since the millennium, I have seen my writing income plummet. Throughout the 1990s, I earned in the low six figures writing about health and sexuality. In 2023, writing made me $12,000. Of that, book royalties came to $1,500. As my writing income fell, of necessity I developed other sources of income. For the past twenty years, I've made my living from real estate, renting apartments in buildings I've acquired. Still, I love to write and continue to pursue my passion daily. I hope to keep writing until I die.

After almost half a century as an author, I'm neither rich nor famous. Chances are you've never heard of me. The Sunday *New York Times* Book Review has never asked me which books sit on my night table. Oh, I've had a few mentions in the *Times*, and I appeared on *Today* and *The Phil Donahue Show* when it was *the* showcase for books. But occasional moments in the sun don't alter the fact that I've spent my career in the shade.

The Untold Story of Books can't tell anyone how to get happily published or pen bestsellers. Instead, I hope this book provides what many authors and book lovers lack: a clear, historically informed understanding of how today's book business evolved and continues to change, and the implications for everyone who writes—and reads—books. I hope this book enriches reading for book lovers and helps authors surf the crashing waves of publishing and write productively, happily, and maybe even gainfully.

Part I

The First Book Business
Hand-Crafted Publishing
From Gutenberg to the End of the
Nineteenth Century

1

Want a Book? That'll Be $75,000

Around Paleolithic campfires, early humans told stories. Some spoke and others listened, commented, and recounted tales of their own. Bathed in firelight, nothing came between those ancient storytellers and their audiences. Everyone was both raconteur and listener. Stories belonged to everyone—until reading, writing, and the copying of words.

Today we view literacy as a foundational skill. But in the ancient world, reading and writing were not only novel, but controversial. Socrates (c. 469–399 BCE) had decidedly mixed feelings about literacy. He recognized its utility in business, government, the military, and the arts, but he argued that writing increased forgetfulness and amplified falsehoods, spurring the dissemination of lies. Ironically, we know how Socrates felt only because his student Plato took notes on his mentor's teachings and published them in the *Phaedrus*.

Echoes of Socrates's sentiments are still with us. During the 1970s, when telephone speed dial was introduced, alarmists warned that users would forget important numbers. And today, everyone decries the avalanche of misinformation available online.

The earliest documents on paperlike materials were rolled into scrolls that filled libraries established by the rulers of ancient empires, particularly Egypt, where the library of Alexandria opened around 300 BCE. It housed the ancient world's largest collection of scrolls, some seven hundred thousand, until conquerors set it ablaze and destroyed everything. Scrolls looked very similar—so similar, in fact, that ancient librarians couldn't tell them apart. To identify them, they affixed tags to scrolls' margins that were called, in Latin, *titulus*—the source of our word "title."

From the dawn of literacy through the first printing press, scribes embraced a variety of media: cuneiform on clay tablets; alphabets and pictographs chiseled in stone or, in China, on bronze plates; and later charcoal or ink on bark, papyrus, parchment (any animal skin), vellum (parchment from calfskin), and eventually paper. But all early reproduction methods shared a common characteristic. Scribes copied books one at a time by hand—in Latin, *manuscript*.

Single-copy reproduction allowed legions of scribes to earn good livings. But it was so laborious that books cost a fortune, in today's dollars around $75,000 per copy, which is the current price for a new scroll of the Hebrew Five Books of Moses (the Torah). A rare holdout of pre-Gutenberg reproduction, the foundational narrative of Judaism is still written by hand on parchment, which takes contemporary scribes one year to copy.

Scrolls left one side blank. During late Roman times, anonymous scribes discovered they could cut materials costs in half if they used both sides. In a technological leap around 100 CE, they began cutting scrolls into rectangular sheets with one side stitched together: codices (singular, "codex"), the precursors of books.

Before Gutenberg, European monk-scribes produced fabulously illustrated codices for kings, the Church, and for Europe's first universities,

Bologna (established in 1088) and Paris (1150). Early books were so valuable that to prevent theft, they were chained to library shelves.

THE WORLD'S FIRST AUTHOR KNOWN BY NAME WAS A WOMAN
She was the Sumerian princess-priestess Enheduanna (2285–2250 BCE), daughter of the Sumerian king Sargon. Most Sumerian priests were men, but apparently an exception was made for the king's daughter. Enheduanna was the high priestess of the moon temple in Ur (the native city of the biblical patriarch Abraham). Cuneiform fragments preserve her name and some of the hymns she wrote. Her writing addressed the goddess of love on behalf of women who pined for mates.

Johannes Gutenberg (c. 1398–1468) was to mechanical printing what, five centuries later, Apple cofounders Steve Jobs and Steve Wozniak were to the personal computer. Jobs and Wozniak did not invent personal computers from scratch. They built on others' work in innovative ways, combining existing technologies—silicon chips, printed circuitry, and video monitors—into something new. Gutenberg did the same. A goldsmith by trade, he didn't dream up movable type. As a young apprentice, he watched master goldsmiths fit short strings of movable metal letters into stamping devices to "sign" their creations. His insight involved applying the idea to printing.

Nor did Gutenberg invent his printing press. He borrowed its design from the devices used since Roman times to extract olive oil. But in 1450, when he adapted those ideas to printing, he changed the world. In one day, a scribe could produce a page or two of text, but a few printers operating a Gutenberg press could crank out hundreds. This marked the first step in the evolution of printing: fewer people making more copies of more books faster and cheaper.

The printing press democratized publishing. During the several thousand years of scribal manuscript creation and copying, scribes worked for rulers, temples, and the economic elite. Ancient scrolls were "published" but not widely disseminated. Most people had no access to them. The printing press changed that, enabling what publishing means today, reproduction of words made available to just about everyone.

Before Gutenberg, Europe housed fewer than ten thousand books. But by 1500, after just sixty years of printing, the number exceeded twenty million pamphlets and books, and by 1600, as printing spread around the world, 150 million.

In just one generation, the printing press threw almost every scribe out of work. Scribes made good money—until the rug got pulled out. Their anguish is lost to history, but imagine if artificial intelligence eliminated all need for teachers, lawyers, and doctors. All technological advances produce winners and losers. We can commiserate with those displaced scribes just as we pity anyone replaced by new technologies today. But who would want to return to hand-copied books priced like luxury automobiles? From day one, book publishers have moved heaven and earth to cut costs.

The printing press spurred literacy and fostered education. It enabled mass communication, ending the political and religious elites' monopoly on information. It allowed translation of the Bible into vernacular languages, which fueled the Reformation. It triggered the Enlightenment, scientific research, and the industrial revolution, and created journalism, often called "the press." And it galvanized dreams of self-determination, which eventually forced most monarchies to yield to parliamentary systems. All because it took fewer people far less time to produce exponentially more copies of reading material. And as $75,000 precious objects faded into the past, a mighty industry developed that required ever-greater amounts of capital to produce ever-cheaper books.

2

Gutenberg Went Bankrupt

Gutenberg had the money to construct a few presses, but he lacked the capital to set up a shop, create type, and buy paper and ink. Around 1450, he borrowed 800 guilders ($75,000 today) at 6 percent interest from fellow goldsmith Johann Furst (c. 1400–1466), who had prospered and become an investor-financier. Two years later, Gutenberg borrowed another 800 guilders from Furst, doubling his debt.

With Furst's investment, Gutenberg printed 180 Bibles and displayed one at a trade fair in Frankfurt. A priest examined it and reported to church authorities that a "marvelous man" had invented a machine that copied text faithfully without scribes. That priest later became Pope Pius II (1405–1464). He called Gutenberg's Bible "extremely neat and legible, not at all difficult to follow."

Almost immediately, Gutenberg's invention was hailed as revolutionary. But at the time, few people were literate, and Gutenberg's Bibles cost so much that hardly anyone could afford them. They sold so poorly that the father of movable type couldn't repay his creditor.

In 1455, Furst sued Gutenberg to recoup his investment. The court ordered Gutenberg to surrender his presses, marking him the first of innumerable publishers to go belly-up. After Furst acquired Gutenberg's presses, he hired Gutenberg's foreman. They made a go of printing by producing brief, inexpensive religious tracts for the Church and single-sheet advertising flyers for local businesses. But not books.

Forty-nine Gutenberg Bibles survive today. Three can be viewed at the Morgan Library in New York. Despite Gutenberg's bankruptcy, his press invented not only publishing but also the far more powerful (and to the elite, scary) idea of mass media.

The Origins of Copyright: Author? What Author?

European monarchs feared (correctly) that Gutenberg's invention might lead to sedition, and the Catholic Church feared (rightly) that printing might lead to heresy on a scale previously unimaginable. Soon kings and bishops were cataloguing material they authorized for reproduction and offering favored printers the exclusive right to copy it—the original incarnation of "copyright." In exchange, the printers vowed not to reproduce anything the authorities found offensive. In 1486, the Republic of Venice granted the world's first copyright to a printer, and during the century afterward, the practice spread throughout Europe.

But early copyrights were little more than fantasies. Our concept of intellectual property was centuries in the future. Folktales, popular songs, and religious and secular texts were universally considered public domain because culture belonged to everyone. Who could assert ownership? Certainly not authors. They didn't own their work. The owners were the printers who reproduced it. In addition, copyrights could be enforced only within single jurisdictions. Meanwhile, rampant smuggling spread books everywhere. When printers anywhere obtained anything with commercial potential, they inked their presses. Today, we call it piracy, but back then it was like picking wildflowers in an open field.

Piracy ran rampant because it skirted censorship and reduced the cost of books—no licensing fees to copyright holders. Meanwhile, the literate few cared little about copyright, less about printers, and nothing about authors. They just wanted books cheap, and printers were happy to provide them, even as they screamed when other printers pirated *their* editions. From the first copyrights to the present day, piracy has been a thread woven through the tapestry of publishing. And for six centuries, information thieves have justified their crime by banging the same two drums:

• *Information should be free.* That is, it can't be owned.

• *Piracy expands your audience.* Consequently, authors should *thank* book pirates.

Authors were powerless to stop piracy, but many decried it. In 1623, John Heminges and Henry Condell published the First Folio of William Shakespeare's plays. Their preface denounced the "surreptitious copies" in which "injurious imposters" had "maimed" and "deformed" their friend's work.

Why Books Have Publisher Pages

European rulers quickly realized that copyright did nothing to stop publication of subversive material. Nervous kings suspected all printers of treason, imprisoned many, and executed at least one. In 1546, Étienne Dolet (1509–1546) published a pamphlet critical of the French monarchy. He was burned at the stake. But for reasons of politics, profit, and the love of books, many printers continued to ink their presses.

In 1557, England's Queen Mary I (1516-1558) decided that suppressing publishing was a losing proposition. She recruited favored printers to police the nascent industry. She granted a monopoly on printing and bookselling to a guild of twenty-one London printers, the Stationers' Company—on two conditions. First, when members registered copyrights with the government, the others pledged not to reprint that material. Second, if company members discovered infringement, they vowed to report the pirates, who faced prison. But English printers turned out to be lousy police, in part because of unbridled book smuggling from Europe and in part because they routinely pirated one another's titles under assumed names.

Next, England tried prior restraint. In 1643, Parliament enacted the Licensing Order, which required writers to submit manuscripts to government censors, who decided if they merited publication. Today, the Licensing Order appears totalitarian, but ironically, two hundred years after Gutenberg, it was the first acknowledgment in Western law that authors had anything to do with books. Printers and authors hated the Licensing Order, and enforcement was problematic. In 1694, Parliament declined to renew it.

The year before the Licensing Order lapsed, in 1693, England's King William III (1650–1702) tried to quash sedition by requiring printers to identify themselves on the first page of anything they printed. How naive. When early printers published anything iffy, they used phony names and addresses. But ever since King William's order, turn the title page and you see the publisher (or "imprint") page.

Authors' intellectual property rights were first recognized in 1710, when Parliament enacted the Copyright Act, dubbed the Statute of Anne (for Queen Anne). Its preamble stated the statute's justification:

"Printers, Booksellers, and other Persons have of late frequently taken the Liberty of Printing, Reprinting, and Publishing [authors' work] without the Consent of the Authors . . . to their very great Detriment, and too often to the Ruin of them and their Families." The Statute of Anne granted authors copyrights to their work for fourteen years.

Printers were appalled. In their view, *they* owned copyrights, not authors. Authors wrote. They copied. The right to copy was theirs. Surprisingly, authors agreed. At the time, the intelligentsia firmly believed that authors wrote not for money, but only for the love of sharing knowledge. Authors of that era considered writing for money dishonorable, a form of intellectual prostitution that carries forward to the present day in the stereotype of iconoclastic writers who abhor book promotion, much to the chagrin of their publishers.

To rescue authors from being labeled harlots, printers graciously offered to take copyrights off their hands. Authors felt fine about this: *I'm published. My name is on the cover. That's what counts.* So, despite the pro-author Statute of Anne, copyrights quickly shifted to printers, and English courts upheld the practice. But after fourteen years, copyrights evaporated and books entered the public domain. Anyone could copy them.

When England's first copyrights expired, their printer-owners howled, insisting that the public domain was sanctioned theft. They argued that, like ownership of land, copyrights should endure forever. Opponents of perpetual copyright countered that it kept books unduly expensive and that, unlike land, ownership of books had to balance copyright holders' right to financial return against the public's right to unfettered idea exchange.

The controversy raged for decades, until Parliament decided once and for all to limit copyright term to fourteen years. This allowed low-cost reprints of public-domain titles, among them, works by Chaucer, Shake-speare, and Milton, which cemented them as canonical.

England also felt threatened by printing in its North American colonies. In 1685, King James II wrote Thomas Dongan, governor of New York, "And for as much a great inconvenience may arise by the liberty of printing within our province of New York, you are to provide by all necessary orders that noe person keep any press for printing, nor that any book, pamphlet or other matters whatsoever bee printed without your special leave & license first obtained."

But by that time, the genie could not be stuffed back into the lamp.

Free Expression, What a Concept!

As Europe's rulers attempted to restrict printing, English intellectuals agitated for a radical new notion: freedom of expression.

In 1644, the year after the enactment of the draconian Licensing Order, John Milton (1608–1674) risked prison by publishing his force-ful protest against censorship, *Areopagitica: A Speech of Mr. John Milton for the Liberty of Unlicensed Printing*. Named for the Areopagus, the Athenian hill where ancient tribunals took place (including the trial of Socrates), *Areopagitica* was the first and among the most impassioned arguments for intellectual freedom. Milton proclaimed, "Give me the liberty to know, to utter, and to argue freely according to conscience, above all liberties. . . . Let [Truth] and Falsehood grapple; who ever knew Truth put to the worse, in a free and open encounter?"

Milton was an idealist. Today, in a world awash in deepfakes and malicious misinformation, we'll forgive poor old Milton for his lack of foresight.

Areopagitica was eloquent, but fifty years passed before Parliament granted freedom of the press in 1695—and then only in England. In the colonies, printer-licensing laws remained in effect, outraging printers, including Benjamin Franklin (1706–1790) and other American revolutionaries, who later enshrined freedom of expression in the First Amendment of the Bill of Rights.

= 3 =

Meanwhile, in America: *Want a Book?* *That'll Be $600*

The first printing press in the Western Hemisphere was established in Mexico City in 1539. It printed church and government documents. A century later, in 1638, America's first printing press arrived in Cambridge, Massachusetts, with one box of type and 240 pounds of paper. It printed religious texts for divinity students at Harvard College (est. 1636), plus handbills, posters, and a few books, notably the *Almanack Calculated for New England.*

Few colonists were literate. The rare colonial home containing any books housed two: a Bible and an almanac (from the Greek word for "calendar"). Almanacs included holidays, tide tables, historical weather records, sunrise and sunset charts, solar and lunar eclipses, recommended planting dates, and proverbs. For colonial printers, almanacs were reliable moneymakers. Unlike Bibles, many buyers purchased them annually. Dozens were published along the East Coast, including *Poor Richard's Almanack* (1732–1758), written and printed in Philadelphia by Ben Franklin under the pen name Richard Saunders ("Early to bed, early to rise. . . ."). The most durable has been *The Old Farmer's Almanac,* published annually and continuously in New Hampshire since 1792, making it North America's oldest periodical. Almanacs were publishing staples until World War I.

THE OLDEST, MOST VALUABLE AMERICAN BOOK

In 1640, two years after its arrival, America's first press printed the Western Hemisphere's first full-length book in English, all 150 psalms in verse, *The Whole Booke of Psalmes*, better known as the Bay Psalm Book. At the time, Massachusetts had no printers, so a locksmith worked the press, poorly. Pages were bound in the wrong order and spelling errors abounded. At the top of each page, the word "psalm" appears—spelled that way on verso pages, but on the recto, it's "psalme." Of the 1,700-copy run, eleven survive, making the Bay Psalm Book scarcer than Gutenberg Bibles (forty-nine) and First Folios of Shakespeare (233). Two landed in the library of Boston's Old South Church, where Benjamin Franklin was baptized. In 2013, one sold for $14 million, the most ever paid for a book.

The colonies imported almost all books from England. They sold for today's equivalent of around $600, more than most colonists earned in a year. If books included diagrams or woodcut illustrations—mostly in medical and scientific texts—they cost up to twice as much.

Six-Hundred-dollar books cost only a small fraction of scribe-copied titles, but even for the elite, they were expensive. To sell them, one Boston printer, Samuel Gerrish (c. 1680s-1741), turned his shop into an after-hours community center for readers and writers. He poured ale and led discussions of current events. When the crowd became sufficiently tipsy to open their wallets, he presented books he'd printed. Gerrish's literary salon attracted several writers, among them the noted Puritan minister Cotton Mather (1663–1728), who later hired the printer to publish a book of his sermons.

Early American books were printed in dark, cramped, noisy shops that reeked of ink and sweat. Printers typeset manuscripts by hand—one letter, punctuation mark, or space at a time—and printed a few pages at a time (folios). Presses clattered as apprentices inked the beds, pulled finished pages, and hung them to dry. Dry pages were folded and trimmed, then sewn together and glued between covers of leather, metal, or wood.

In today's terms, colonial printers were actually printer-publisher-booksellers. They performed all three functions. Book advertising, if any, was limited to displays in shop windows and brief notices in periodicals the printers published. If buyers elsewhere ordered books, printers shipped them by wagon or boat, or sent them with travelers headed that way.

Printing was a risky business and many shops failed. To survive, Ben Franklin competed furiously with Philadelphia's other printers. In the periodicals he published, Franklin used pseudonyms to deride the competition. In 1728, writing as "Martha Careful," Franklin threatened to throttle rival printer Samuel Keimer (1689–1742) for daring to publish an article sympathetic to abortion: "In behalf of my Self and many good modest Women in this City . . . a Warning to Samuel Keimer: That if he proceed farther to Expose the Secrets of our Sex, in That audacious manner . . . my Sister Molly and my Self, with some others, are Resolved to run the Hazard of taking him by the Beard, at the next Place we meet him, and make an Example of him."

Franklin was by no means alone. Throughout the colonies, printer-publisher-booksellers used noms de plume to laud their own output while ridiculing that of other printers. Like Samuel Gerrish, Franklin hosted salons and courted writers, hoping they would hire him to print their books. Franklin landed a big fish when an itinerant minister popular at religious revivals selected him to publish a book of sermons. The book sold so well—over a few years, more than one thousand copies—that Franklin was able to step back from his clattering presses and devote much of his time to politics, diplomacy, and scientific research.

In 1775, the Continental Congress named Franklin the colonies' first postmaster general. He developed a postal rate structure that granted discounts to periodicals and books, in part because he believed that a democracy should subsidize idea exchange. But Franklin was no fool. Postal discounts also subsidized his business. The U.S. Postal Service still grants discounts to "media mail."

America's First "Public" Library

When young Ben Franklin opened his print shop, only clergy and literate parishioners had access to church libraries. Book collections at the few colonial colleges were restricted to students and faculty. And only the richest colonists owned any books. This frustrated Franklin, who yearned to read more books than he could print, buy, or borrow.

He recruited friends to pool their meager collections and chip in for additional volumes and a place to house them. It wasn't easy. From Franklin's autobiography: "So few were the readers at that time in Philadelphia, and the majority of us so poor, that I was not able, with great industry, to find more than fifty persons, mostly young tradesmen, willing to pay."

But Franklin persisted. In 1731, he founded the Library Company of Philadelphia. Neither tax supported nor free to users, it was not a true public library. (The first opened a century later in Boston.) But Franklin's library was open to anyone willing to pay the modest annual fee. It was America's first public-access library—in fact, the nation's first cultural institution.

From the American Revolution until 1800, the Library Company housed the Library of Congress. It was the country's largest library until the Civil War. Today the Library Company is almost three hundred years old and archives some seven hundred thousand books and historical manuscripts.

Meanwhile, Elsewhere . . .

As printing spread around the world, it spurred social change. Widely circulated pamphlets by the philosophers John Locke (1632–1704) and Jean-Jacques Rousseau (1712–1778) promoted the "social contract," the idea that governments ruled not by autocratic decrees but through laws embraced by the governed. Their ideas resonated particularly in France, where pamphlets mocked France's last king, Louis XVI, and his queen, Marie Antoinette. The printing press helped foment the French Revolution of 1789.

Paper arrived in the Arab world from China before it appeared in Europe. When movable type reached the region, sultans from Morocco to Persia prohibited printing, fearing that sacrilegious printers might alter the Quran. Consequently, the first printed Quran was produced in Venice between 1537 and 1538.

Wherever printing presses appeared, they generated controversy, rather like today's bruhaha over generative artificial intelligence.

4

How to Reduce the Price of Books: Piracy

By 1650, American printers were churning out advertising handbills and cheap periodicals and pamphlets galore, but few full-length books. Books were still very expensive—and would have cost even more had American printers paid English copyright holders for reprint rights. They didn't. When ships from England docked at American ports, printers pirated the books they brought to these shores.

Boston boasted the most printers. By the 1660s, they routinely condemned one another for releasing pirate editions of books they themselves had stolen. Eventually, they negotiated an agreement pledging not to reprint what others had released. But there was no honor among thieves, not to mention that printers outside Boston eagerly pirated every book that came their way. English authors and printers rarely learned of colonial reprints and received nothing. American readers didn't care about intellectual property rights. They coveted books and wanted them as inexpensive as possible.

By 1673, it became clear that Boston's printers were too mercenary to maintain any gentleman's agreement, so the Massachusetts colonial legislature granted five-year copyrights to the first printers to publish books, including pirated English titles. But the statute applied only in the Bay State. Printers elsewhere continued to pirate freely, among them Ben Franklin. In 1740, he bootlegged what many scholars consider the first novel in English, *Pamela; or, Virtue Rewarded*, by Samuel Richardson (1689–1761).

Women Discover a Passion for Books

Richardson's father hoped his son would become a minister but couldn't afford divinity school tuition. Richardson loved to read and decided to become a printer. He lived at the dawn of England's industrial revolution, a time when hordes of country peasants began migrating to the country's burgeoning cities to work in its new factories or, in the case of many young women, as domestics in the homes of affluent burghers.

Richardson was a born writer. Friends suggested he might do well writing and printing a handbook for country girls headed for urban factory work or domestic service—with an emphasis on avoiding employers' sexual harassment. Richardson's wife suggested that a fictional tale might work better than a how-to. The result was *Pamela*, the story of a naive but clever country girl who enters domestic service and endures threatened and actual rape by her crass employer, before ultimately winning his love and turning him into a devoted husband.

With literacy rising quickly in industrializing Britain, English women went crazy for *Pamela*, which quickly became wildly successful. Printers were amazed how many women wanted to read stories about girls like themselves overcoming adversity to win the love of rich, powerful, charismatic men. Other authors—as far as we know, all men—penned similar tales, and printer-publishers rushed them into print.

Pamela was more than the first English novel and fiction bestseller. It also invented the romance fiction genre. It turned huge numbers of women into avid readers and many into writers. Today romance fiction ranks as the perennial top-selling category of fiction. Women write the vast majority of it. Women also buy two-thirds of all books and three-quarters of all fiction.

Fifteen years after *Pamela*'s appearance, a different kind of redemption story emerged for a much different audience: not women, but children. It featured the debut of a girl nicknamed Goody Two-Shoes. The original Goody was not insufferably virtuous. She was, rather, the feisty, resourceful protagonist of the Cinderella story *The History of Little Goody Two-Shoes* (1765), the first novel in English directed at young or juvenile ("juvie") readers, from middle schoolers to young adults. Its author remains unknown, but scholars attribute the book to the Irish writer Oliver Goldsmith (1728–1774).

At the time of its publication, children's literature consisted of fairy tales and Aesop's Fables. *Goody Two-Shoes* was much grittier. The little sister of romance fiction, it tells the rags-to-riches tale of young Margery Meanwell, a girl so poor she has only one shoe. When her fortunes improve, she acquires another and becomes so excited she earns the nickname Goody Two-Shoes. Like romance heroines, Goody stands in marked contrast to the gender roles of eighteenth-century England. She teaches herself to read, foils a robbery, founds a school for poor children, and overcomes accusations of witchcraft.

The book was wildly popular, a favorite of boys as well as girls. It appeared in dozens of editions in England and many more pirated editions in the colonies. Jane Austen (1775–1817) cherished it and kept her childhood copy until her death. The *Harry Potter* books, *Mary Poppins*, the *Chronicles of Narnia*, and much of today's juvenile fiction owe a debt to the not-at-all-overly virtuous little girl with one shoe.

Entrepreneurial Authors Hire Printers

Upper-crust colonial book buyers considered England the center of the cultural universe and raced to buy fashionable English titles. American printers naturally invested their labor and materials in pirating English books. But printers had far less incentive to risk capital on American authors. When homegrown writers sought publication, printers said, *Sure, we'll print—if you pay for it.* So American authors financed printing. All early American books were author- (or patron-) financed. In current parlance, they were self-published.

Why pay to publish? Colonial-era writers were just like today's authors. They loved books and reading. They had something to say. They yearned to see their names on title pages. And if they wanted to publish, their only option was to hire printers.

For early American authors, writing was not a profession but a sideline. Washington Irving (1783–1859) was a lawyer. James Fenimore Cooper (1789–1851) sailed with the U.S. Navy. Nathaniel Hawthorne (1804–1864) was a customs agent. Ralph Waldo Emerson (1803–1882) and Henry Wadsworth Longfellow (1807–1882) were teachers. Oliver Wendell Holmes (1809–1894) practiced medicine. Henry David Thoreau (1817–1862) worked in his family's pencil factory. And Louisa May Alcott (1832–1888) was a governess. Like most authors today, they wrote for love, and if they made a little money, usually from speaking engagements, they considered it gravy.

Meanwhile, colonial printers enjoyed a sweet deal publishing author-financed books. They made a profit on every title. One was Daniel Henchman (1689–1761) of Boston, whose records survive. When authors engaged his services, Henchman took eight weeks to produce fifty copies. Most went to the author while some stayed with him. Henchman adorned his shop's windows with titles he'd published, and if any sold, he agreed to split the proceeds with the authors.

But it's virtually certain that Henchman neglected to split the income as promised. Royalty theft was not only easy, but it was also protected by law. Authors had no right to audit printers, so they never knew how many copies were printed, how many were sold, and how much printers owed them. In addition, if books caught on, printers were free to reprint them ad infinitum without informing authors or paying a cent.

Authors on both sides of the Atlantic assumed that printers cheated them, among them the big-name English author Samuel Johnson (1709–1784). His popular *A Dictionary of the English Language* (1755) defined "pirate" as "any robber; particularly a bookseller who seizes the copies of other men."

Authors made most of their money not from printer payments but from sales in the back of the room after lectures. Authors warehoused their books in their homes and brought them to speaking gigs. Thoreau kept boxes of his debut title, *A Week on the Concord and Merrimack Rivers* (1849), in his cottage and didn't sell many. In his diary, he noted: "I have now a library of nearly nine hundred volumes, over seven hundred of which I wrote myself."

THE ORIGIN OF BOOK DEDICATIONS

Immediately following the publisher page, virtually all books include dedications. The custom began in ancient Rome, where many authors could not afford to finance the copying of their scrolls and dedicated their work to the generous patrons who did.

But patrons were scarce. In *Tristam Shandy* by Laurence Sterne (1713–1768), Shandy can't find a backer for his book. Instead of a dedication, he substituted: "To be let [sold] for fifty guineas."

Centuries later during the second book business, as publishers assumed manufacturing costs, dedications evolved into what they are today, appreciations of those authors hold dear.

5

Copyright Struggles and Printing Innovations, as Pulp Paper Creates an Enduring Class Divide in Books

By the second half of the eighteenth century, authors decided that maybe it was okay to earn money writing books. They also realized that printers couldn't be trusted and decided that if they paid to publish, they should hold copyrights.

In 1770, the Boston choirmaster William Billings (1746–1800) set biblical verses to original music and hired a printer to publish his *New-England Psalm-Singer*, which was quickly pirated. Hoping to save the sequel from the same fate, Billings persuaded the Massachusetts legislature to grant its copyright to him. However, Governor Thomas Hutchinson vetoed the bill, citing the English practice of printers holding them.

The seed Billings planted sprouted during the American Revolution as prominent writers agitated for author copyrights, among them the political firebrand Thomas Paine (1737–1809) and especially Noah Webster (1758–1843). Today, we remember Webster for his dictionary, *A Compendious Dictionary of the English Language* (1806), or *Webster's*. But for decades before that book appeared, he ranked among the new nation's top authors, thanks to his three-volume literacy text, *A Grammatical Institute of the English Language*, which included a speller (1783), grammar (1784), and reader (1785).

Naturally, Webster's books were pirated as quickly as printers could set type. As he traveled the country promoting literacy and selling his work, he found illicit copies of his books everywhere and advocated tough copyright laws to protect authors. He organized writers to petition the Continental Congress, proclaiming "that nothing is more properly a man's own than the fruit of his study, and that the protection and security of literary property would greatly tend to encourage genius [and] to promote useful discoveries." (At the time, "genius" meant creativity.)

But under the loose Articles of Confederation, the newly independent states were sovereign and Congress had little sway. Nonetheless, the delegates supported author copyright and passed a resolution urging the states to "secure to the authors . . . copyright of such books for a certain time, not less than fourteen years from the first publication."

With congressional resolution in hand, Webster returned home to Connecticut and, in 1783, engineered passage of the nation's first true copyright law. It granted the state's authors "the sole liberty of printing, publishing and vending" their books for fourteen years, with one fourteen-year extension. It also created a book registration system and enacted severe penalties for piracy.

Webster hailed the law but objected to its time limit. He advocated perpetual copyright, arguing as English printers had that his books should be his forever. But Webster was outmaneuvered. Printers favored time-limited copyrights. As they expired and books entered the public domain, anyone could reprint them. Intellectuals also supported the time limit to encourage idea exchange. And the majority of the population, illiterate anti-intellectuals, saw no reason to protect authors at all, let alone grant perpetual ownership of anything as frivolous as words.

Meanwhile, Webster's copyright law applied only in Connecticut. It was essentially meaningless. Books copyrighted there were immediately pirated elsewhere.

In 1789, when the states ratified the Constitution, Article 1, Section 8 specified: "The Congress shall have Power To . . . promote the Progress of Science and useful Arts, by securing for limited Times to Authors and Inventors the exclusive Right to their respective Writings and Discoveries." Writers and inventors are the only two occupations specifically granted Constitutional protection.

Soon after, the first U.S. Congress enacted the Copyright Act of 1790. Taken almost verbatim from the Statute of Anne, it required registration of books with what eventually became the U.S. Copyright Office and granted a single term of fourteen years.

The Copyright Act also flipped a post-revolutionary middle finger at England. It specifically protected American piracy of English books: "Nothing in this Act shall be construed to prohibit the . . . reprinting or publishing within the United States, of any map, chart, book or books, written, printed, or published by any person not a citizen of the United States."

Ironically, American authors greeted the Copyright Act with a collective shrug. During its first decade, Americans published some thirteen thousand books and pamphlets but copyrighted only 556.

Why so few? Early authors assumed rampant piracy, so compared with today's writers, they felt less sense of ownership. In addition, copyright violations could be remedied only through litigation, but very few books sold well enough to justify it. Finally, if authors won verdicts in one state, printers elsewhere could still pirate them, so why bother?

Innovation Drives Printing and Publishing

By 1800, the U.S. population topped five million, two million of whom could read. America's biggest book town was Boston, population 25,000, with thirty booksellers, mostly printers, but also stationery shops, schools, churches, and dry goods stores (forerunners of department stores). The number two book town was Philadelphia, population 40,000, with sixteen booksellers, followed by New York (60,000 and thirteen); Charleston, South Carolina (15,000 and three); and Baltimore, Maryland (26,000 and one). The biggest sellers continued to be Bibles, sermon collections, and almanacs. But Americans showed increasing interest in books dealing with science, politics, medicine, and music—and women continued to adore novels, particularly romance fiction and multigeneration family sagas.

Growing demand for books spurred innovations that once again allowed fewer people to produce more copies of more titles faster and cheaper. One advance involved type. Until the 1720s, it had to be imported from England because the colonies had no foundries. Ben Franklin established the nation's first, which cut printers' costs. In recognition, in 1902, America's typographers named a popular sans serif font after him: Franklin Gothic.

Another advance involved press design. From 1440 through the eighteenth century, wooden screw presses were state of the art. Franklin's press looked much like Gutenberg's. But wood parts wore out and limited the pressure that could be applied, compromising quality. In 1810, the first iron presses improved reproduction quality and quadrupled print speed to five hundred sheets an hour. By the Civil War, subsequent innovations raised it to an astonishing twenty thousand pages an hour—

forty times more in just sixty minutes than a scribe could copy in a year. As press speeds increased, the cost of books dropped.

Paper also evolved. Before Gutenberg, scribes wrote on parchment, livestock skins beaten into thin sheets. Parchment was very costly: each book required a herd of animals. The printing press spurred a quest for cheaper alternatives. Europeans discovered that excellent paper could be produced inexpensively from hemp and flax, the source of linen. The Pilgrims introduced both plants to North America, but the colonies had no paper mills, so every sheet had to be imported. The first American mill opened in 1690 in Philadelphia, eventually ending colonial dependence on English paper.

In 1794, Eli Whitney (1765–1825) patented his cotton "gin," short for "engine," which pulled the seeds from cotton puffs so efficiently that the fiber quickly became the South's leading export. Cotton, wool, and rags could be chopped and boiled into a slurry, then pressed into low-cost paper, which reduced printer-publishers' costs.

By the Civil War, as presses became faster and more complicated, printing and bookbinding diverged. Printers presented loose folios to newly independent bookbinders, who sewed and glued them between leather covers, which became standard.

But glues were unreliable. Books often fell apart. In 1808, the Bostonian Elijah Upton introduced a cheap, dependable glue that solved the problem. In 1832, another Boston bookbinder popularized covers and spines of cloth-wrapped cardboard, much cheaper than leather. And a Philadelphia company developed a quick, inexpensive way to glue metal foil. Within a decade, most book covers and spines boasted shiny, eye-catching titles in metal leaf.

These advances further reduced book prices, transforming them from luxuries for the rich into upscale consumer items within reach of the small but growing upper middle class. Still, books remained expensive, typically costing three dollars (around $100 today).

Mathew Carey: Book Pioneer

By 1800, U.S. printers used American paper and type but still relied on imported ink. In 1803, the Philadelphia printer Mathew Carey (1760–1839) organized fellow printers to offer a fifty-dollar prize ($1,500 today) for the best American-made ink. An amateur chemist won and launched a company to produce his invention. Printers soon used nothing else.

Carey's group also offered a prize for the best paper made from a new material. The winner used sawdust from lumber mills. Almost overnight, wood pulp became the source of coarse but remarkably cheap paper. European printers quickly embraced pulp paper, and America, with its vast forests, gained a valuable export.

Finally, Carey introduced proofreading. Early American books were typically typeset by young, poorly schooled apprentices, who infuriated authors by introducing typos and misspellings. Starting around 1790, Carey printed test pages, "proofs," and corrected them before final printing. Proofreading required extra paper, ink, and labor, raising costs, which led competing printers to cluck, *Authors will never pay for it*. But error-free books proved so popular that authors flocked to Carey, and proofreading became standard.

Colonial Printers vs. Early Booksellers

Bigger, faster printing presses using cheaper ink on cheaper paper allowed more copies of more books to be produced at lower cost per copy. The number of books rose and prices fell. This was a boon to book buyers, but it forced printer-publishers to invest more in equipment, which pinched their margins, driving some out of business. Periodic financial panics ruined others. And in Boston, New York, and Philadelphia, where competition was most intense, some printers resorted to arson to destroy their rivals.

As the industry became more competitive, increasingly larger printer-publishers became increasingly concerned with book marketing and distribution. Printers clustered in large towns, but 95 percent of Americans lived on farms often many days' journey from the nearest print shop. Roads were poor. Shipping was costly and unreliable. How could printer-publishers sell books effectively outside their home regions?

In 1806, when Webster published his *Dictionary*, in addition to selling through his printer, he organized the nation's first book sales force. At the time, an army of peddlers hiked the lanes of rural America selling household items, Bibles, almanacs, and books of sermons by prominent clergy. Webster sold distribution rights to select peddlers, granting each a territory. This launched a fifty-year period when peddlers carried books far and wide, usually on foot with packs on their backs. But books were heavy. Selection was limited.

Back in the towns, printers displayed only the books they printed. To see all available titles, buyers had to trudge from shop to shop. Sensing an opportunity, a few entrepreneurs opened stores that offered many printers' titles. As bookshops became fixtures in major coastal towns, printers gradually exited retailing in favor of wholesaling to the new booksellers.

Early bookstores resembled today's used bookshops: small, cramped, quirky, and off the beaten track where rent was low. They bought stock at 30 to 50 percent off the cover or "list" price. (Today, the standard wholesale discount is typically at least 50 percent off list.) Early booksellers also offered writing supplies: quill pens, paper, ink, and blank books for diaries, at that time very popular.

Printer-publishers loved booksellers in theory but in practice often found them exasperating. The few bookshops couldn't collectively sell titles as quickly as printers produced them. Booksellers retorted that printer-publishers treated them less like allies than adversaries. Printers refused to ship on credit. They insisted on cash up front. And they didn't accept returns on purchased inventory, which limited what booksellers could afford to stock. Booksellers also complained that printers shipped so haphazardly that many copies arrived too damaged to sell, a loss booksellers had to eat.

One printer critical of bookshops' "failures" was the enterprising Mathew Carey. In 1802, he rented a banquet room at a popular New York City restaurant and invited printers throughout the Northeast to sell their books directly to consumers—America's first book fair. Around the country, in schools, hotel ballrooms, and church social halls, book fairs quickly became popular multiday events. Printers offered as many titles as they could ship. Smart buyers attended twice: early the first day for the greatest selection and late the final day to pick up leftovers cheap.

Book fairs enthralled everyone—except booksellers, who denounced them as business killers: *You printers have no business in retailing.* Printers retorted, *You booksellers don't move enough titles. If you can't get the job done . . .*

Pulp Paper Creates an Enduring Class Divide in Books

During the eighteenth century, women continued to inhale romance fiction, while increasingly literate Americans loved novels, gobbling up instant classics like *Robinson Crusoe* (1719) and *Gulliver's Travels* (1726). In addition, hordes of men (and some women) read *Memoir of a Woman of Pleasure*, aka *Fanny Hill* (1748), the first pornographic novel in English. But for much of the population, one copy of a novel on cotton-linen paper between leather covers cost several months' wages.

Then wood-pulp paper appeared. American printer-publishers were slow to adopt it, but their English counterparts saw money in the bank. They released cheap wood-pulp paperbacks for the working class for just 10 percent of the price of leather-bound books. Laborers loved them and pulp paperbacks sold like crazy, which spurred American printer-publishers to follow suit. Meanwhile, affluent buyers of "quality" books derided the new format as "pulp fiction" and "penny dreadfuls," snooty terms that marked the beginning of a lasting class division between princely highbrow literature and its bastard pulp cousin.

Pulp paper arrived as the industrial revolution began to turn agricultural peasants into urban factory workers. After the Civil War, American industrialization created great wealth for the few and social upheaval for everyone. The period from 1870 through the close of the nineteenth century became known as the Gilded Age, but the gilding was a thin veneer over orphaned children, child labor, criminal gangs, overcrowded tenements, sanitation nightmares, virulent epidemics, drug addiction, and Dickensian working conditions.

Out of this volatile stew, the upper class of the young United States established, in the words of the Yale professor Alan Trachtenberg, "a particular idea of culture as a privileged domain of refinement, aesthetic sensibility, and higher learning." Culture was no longer the sum total of a people's stories but just those that resonated for the elite, who viewed lower-class sensibilities as boorish.

The arbiters of Gilded Age gentility touted their vision of culture as an antidote to the ravages of industrialization, a way to civilize the proletariat. It's no coincidence that this era marked the founding of many colleges, museums, orchestras, and opera and ballet companies. Nor is it an accident that upper-class moralists condemned cheap paperbacks for their vulgarity and pernicious influence on the laboring class.

Despite upper-crust hand-wringing, pulp titles proved wildly popular, and the book business changed again. As books became cheaper and coarser, they evolved into everyday consumer items. The grandeur evaporated. In the words of Michael Korda, former editor in chief of Simon & Schuster, "We sell books, other people sell shoes. What's the difference?"

Then Irwin Beadle (1826–1882) out-pulped the pulp publishers. The New York entrepreneur introduced hundred-page novellas on coarse pulp paper for just ten cents ($3): detective and horror stories, lusty romances, action-packed adventure yarns, and shocking exposés of patrician villainy and plebian mayhem. "Books for the Million!" Beadle's advertising proclaimed. "A dollar book for a dime!!" His output became a sensation among the working class—and vastly outsold leather-bound books.

On both sides of the Atlantic, pulp fiction's success galled the elite. *Publishers Weekly* declared that it "degraded literature." Others railed that penny dreadfuls debased prose, corrupted youth, and caused crime. Dime novels sold in the millions.

Then Frank Munsey (1854–1925), owner of *Argosy* magazine, out-pulped Irwin Beadle. He used even coarser, cheaper paper to undersell everyone. He published full-length romance and action-adventure tales for just five cents ($1.50). Munsey's books contained no illustrations, not even on their flimsy covers, and their bindings didn't last long. But readers loved them, and other publishers rushed into the niche. Escapist stories remain popular today—in print and on every streaming service.

Pulp novels sold huge numbers—but *not* in bookshops. Booksellers identified with the gentry and served only the "carriage trade," buyers who arrived not on foot or by bicycle or public transportation but in private carriages. Booksellers refused to stock anything but leather-bound titles. Meanwhile, owners of newsstands and candy and dry goods stores happily offered pulp books, which remained hugely popular until World War II, when government rationing of wood pulp destroyed the genre. After the war, pulp fiction yielded to its better-manufactured descendant, the mass-market paperback (more in Part II).

Literary novels and pulp fiction occupied oddly parallel universes. The former were reviewed, the latter not. Leather-bound books sold modestly but found their way into libraries, sermons, and school curricula. Pulp titles sold in vastly greater numbers but were considered at best ephemeral and at worst corrupting. Successful literary authors were staples of the lecture circuit, while most successful pulp authors remained anonymous. The few exceptions included Zane Grey (1872–1939), whose ninety action-packed westerns sold forty million copies, and Louis L'Amour (1908–1988), whose eighty-nine westerns sold 320 million.

The class divide between high- and lowbrow literature remained central to the book business until the mid-1950s, when bookstores finally embraced paperbacks. But Gilded Age sensibilities linger. Educators continue to tout reading as the expressway to success, and many among the literary elite still scorn pulp's descendants, today's genre fiction: romance, mystery, thrillers, fantasy, westerns, true crime, sci-fi, action-adventure, and erotica.

Finally, the class divide helped reduce the price of books. Pulp fiction sold for pennies and was wildly popular with everyone except the intelligentsia. Price-cutting clearly boosted sales. Publishers bent over backward to cut costs so they could drop the price of books while still making money.

6

New York Becomes the Nation's Publishing Capital on "The Night Before Christmas"

Recall the last time you moved. Packing, hauling, unpacking. What a hassle. Since you're reading this book, you've probably wrestled with moving boxes of books. They're so dang heavy.

Early printer-publishers faced the same problem. Heavy books cost a great deal to ship. Even as technological innovations reduced manufacturing costs, shipping remained cumbersome and expensive. In 1800, Boston and Philadelphia were the top book-producing cities, with more populous New York a distant third. But after 1825, almost overnight, the Big Apple became the nation's publishing capital—thanks to the Erie Canal.

Running 363 miles from the Hudson River to Lake Erie, the Erie Canal was a technological marvel. Its thirty-six locks and elevation change of 565 feet both set world records. The canal provided the first direct waterway from the Atlantic to the Great Lakes and dramatically reduced shipping costs to America's vast interior. Today, Boston and Philadelphia remain publishing centers, but by 1840, New York City's position at the confluence of its harbor and the Hudson River, with the canal only a modest distance away, made it the nation's undisputed printing and publishing powerhouse.

Despite its great benefit, the Erie Canal could not escape winter. Each year, it froze. Combining this limitation with shippers' bulk discounts, publishers shipped large batches of books shortly before the freeze for fall and winter reading, then shipped again shortly after the thaw for spring and summer reading. As a result, publishers organized their catalogues into two seasons, fall and spring.

Two-season publishing became an anachronism after the Civil War, when railroads offered efficient shipping year-round. But today most publishers still organize their catalogues seasonally, with titles by big-name authors released in the fall for Christmas giving.

"Pretty Books" Transform Christmas

Speaking of Christmas, in the early nineteenth century it was nothing like today's ho-ho-holiday. As the historian Stephen Nissenbaum documents in *The Battle for Christmas*, St. Nicholas, aka Santa Claus, was entirely absent, and presents, if any, consisted of homemade pies, cakes, and jams. From colonial times through the 1820s, Christmas was largely a time of tipsy public revelry. In farming communities and small villages, the partying was all in good fun, but as New York grew from a town into a city, Christmas acquired a sinister edge as gangs of drunk hooligans roamed the streets committing vandalism, robbery, and assault. The affluent felt threatened and decided to transform the rowdy holiday into a quiet, indoor family celebration, with gifts for the children.

A key harbinger of this shift was an 1823 poem by Clement Clarke Moore (1779–1863), "A Visit from St. Nicholas" or "The Night Before

Christmas." Borrowing from Dutch colonial tradition, he transformed St. Nick from a stern disciplinarian into Santa Claus, the jovial gent laden with presents.

Moore was an intellectual, a professor at the New York Episcopal Seminary, who saw no point giving children toys when their minds could be improved. His poem, originally "Old Santeclaus," contains this stanza:

No drums to stun their Mother's ear,
Nor swords to make their sisters fear;
But pretty books to store their mind
With knowledge of each various kind.

"Pretty books" caught on. By 1830, printers were churning out gift books for Christmas, and booksellers displayed them prominently. Of course, at the time, books were expensive, especially those made pretty with lavish illustrations. But hey, it was Christmas, and beautifully illustrated volumes became staples of gift giving. This marked the start of Christmas as a commercialized holiday—and the custom of giving books. To this day, the period from Thanksgiving to Christmas is the top time for book sales. Barnes & Noble does one-third of its annual business during those four weeks. Women buy most books. Across B&N's six hundred stores, men outnumber them on just one day each year: Christmas Eve.

P.S. Clement Moore owned a farm on Manhattan's rural west side. As New York grew, the city annexed it. He subdivided, sold lots, and developed the neighborhood that still bears his farm's name, Chelsea.

Before the Civil War: The Worst of Times—and the Best

During the two decades before the Civil War, the book business thrived. By 1850, the United States had one of the largest literate populations on Earth, and tax-supported public education meant more readers every day. In the words of the historian S. H. Steinberg, the mid-nineteenth century represented "a sudden leap forward" that transformed publishing, spurred reading, and created new demand for books.

In 1857, *Harper's New Monthly Magazine* observed that the past decade had witnessed "unparalleled demand [for books]. Presses have been working day and night." And a trade newsletter, the *American Publishers' Circular and Literary Gazette*, declared: "In less than fifty years, publishing houses have arisen in this country from the smallest imaginable beginnings to a magnitude of opulence that is almost incredible."

As the nineteenth century progressed, authors continued to hire printer-publishers, and the book business attracted new entrepreneurs, many of whose names remain familiar today:

• In 1807, the New York printer Charles Wiley (c. 1782–1826) founded the house that still bears the Wiley name.

• In 1817, James Harper (1795–1869) and his brother John (1797–1875) opened a New York print shop, J. & J. Harper, and, as a sideline, published Bibles. Brothers Fletcher (1806–1877) and Joseph Wesley (1801–1870) joined the company. In 1825, Harper & Brothers became a trade publisher.

• In 1836, the Philadelphian Joshua Ballinger Lippincott (1813–1886) began publishing Bibles as J. B. Lippincott & Company, then expanded into trade books.

•The Boston printers William Ticknor (1810–1864) and James T. Fields (1817–1881) continued the tradition of bookshop as community center at their Old Corner Bookstore, which still stands in downtown Boston. Most of the building was a printing plant, but on the ground floor, the partners hosted literary salons that attracted such authors as Emerson, Hawthorne, Longfellow, and Thoreau, all of whom hired T&F to publish their books.

•In 1837, the Bostonians Charles Coffin Little (1799–1869) and James Brown (1800–1855) bought a small legal publisher. In 1847, it became Little, Brown & Company.

•In 1840, Charles Little's son hired George Palmer Putnam (1814–1872) as an apprentice to sweep the shop. In 1838, he became a partner in Wiley & Putnam, then in 1848, launched G. Putnam Broadway. When he died, his three sons inherited the firm, renaming it G. P. Putnam's Sons.

•In the 1850s, the Vermonter Henry Oscar Houghton (1823–1895) worked at a Boston shop that printed books for Little, Brown. In 1864, he partnered with George Mifflin (1845–1921) to form Houghton Mifflin.

•In 1858, the Boston printer William Rand (1828–1915) moved to Chicago and opened a shop with Andrew McNally (1836-1904). Chicago was a rail hub. Their first books were travel guides financed by railroads to encourage travel. Rand McNally became synonymous with travel resources.

•In 1872, the New York lawyer James Shaw Baker (1836–1904) joined a publishing house that became Baker & Taylor. B&T eventually left publishing for book wholesaling. Today it's the leading distributor to school and public libraries.

All these printer-publishers were businessmen who kept both eyes glued to the bottom line. They were also readers who loved the cultural cachet of publishing books. It made them tastemakers and opinion leaders. They had ink under their fingernails, but publishing books conferred prestige—and helped cement New York City as the nation's cultural capital.

Today, most of these houses survive in name only as imprints, wholly owned subsidiaries of the Big Five publishers.

7

Authors Battle Book Piracy as the First Book Sells a Million Copies

The British historian Henry William Herbert (1807–1858) explained that before the Civil War, American publishing found itself "in the midst of a mechanical and economic revolution. . . . Like most periods of rapid and chaotic expansion, it was characterized by greed, ruthlessness, and small heed to the fundamental decencies of civilized business relations." The American historian John Tebbel (1912–2004) put it more succinctly, calling pre–Civil War book publishing the "Age of Piracy." Its main victims were English authors and publishers, who wailed about theft by the damn Yankees but were powerless to stop it.

After 1830, printing and publishing split into separate businesses. Publishers continued to own presses but hired printers to run them, focusing instead on acquiring new titles—largely through more proactive piracy. Instead of waiting for books to emerge from the holds of ships in major ports, publishers sent small boats to fetch them from transatlantic freighters before they docked. As competition increased, they sent agents to Fleet Street, the heart of London publishing, where, in the words of one observer, they "hovered like vultures." The moment new titles appeared the agents sent them across the Atlantic on the fastest vessels available.

Book Piracy 2.0:
From Opportunism to Organized Crime

The most swashbuckling American book pirates were the nation's two biggest publishers, Mathew Carey (whose company evolved into today's Lippincott Williams & Wilkins) and his larger competitor, Harper & Brothers (now HarperCollins). John Tebbel called Harper "unquestionably" America's "leading [book] pirate."

In 1823, Carey wrote his London agent: "28 hours after receiving [the book you sent], we had 1500 copies . . . distributed. . . . In two days we shall publish it here [Philadelphia] and in New York, and the Pirates may print it as soon as they please. The opposition Edition will be out in about 48 hours after they have one of our Copies but we shall have complete and entire possession of every market in the Country for a short time."

Carey shocked London publishers by dispatching his agent to visit them. It was as if Blackbeard's lieutenant had knocked on the door of Buckingham Palace. The agent explained that American piracy could not be stopped, so why not profit from it? His offer: sell page proofs exclusively to Carey. But the amount he offered was insultingly low. *We'll pirate your books either way. Take it or leave it.*

The English figured a pittance was better than nothing. In 1835, an English publisher sold Carey an advance copy of *Rienzi, the Last of the Roman Tribunes,* by the big-name author Edward Bulwer-Lytton (1803–1873). It was the sequel to his immensely popular *The Last Days of Pompeii* (1834), which became a classic movie in 1935. When *Rienzi* arrived in Philadelphia, Carey distributed pages to several printers who worked all night, each printing part of the book. By morning, five hundred copies were collated, bound, boxed, and loaded on stagecoaches.

But when *Rienzi* arrived in New York City, Carey learned the book was already on sale. Its English publisher was not stupid. The house also sold page proofs to Harper. In letters, Bulwer-Lytton mentioned receiving some money from Harper for advance pages, but as a big name, he was the exception. When English publishers sold page proofs, the vast majority of authors received nothing.

Meanwhile, printers on the American frontier stationed *their* agents in Boston, New York, and Philadelphia. When new titles appeared—both American and English—they sent them to Pittsburgh, Detroit, Chicago, and especially Cincinnati, where they were immediately pirated so far away from the East Coast that few copyright holders ever knew.

Eventually, the Harpers realized that their costly guerrilla war with Carey was bad for business. Fletcher Harper negotiated a truce. His "Harper Rule" echoed previous gentleman's agreements, awarding "ownership" of pirated books to the first American publisher to print them. Other publishers pledged not to release competing editions as a "courtesy of the trade." But nineteenth-century publishers were anything but courteous. Harper and Carey continued to pirate each other.

Authors Step into the Fray

During the first book business—that is, until World War I—manufacturing accounted for around one-third of books' retail price, booksellers' markup another third. Printer-publishers and authors split the final third, creating a royalty rate of 16.5 percent. In addition, authors could make money buying copies wholesale and selling them retail after appearances. But few if any authors earned the putative royalty rate. Printer-publishers routinely underreported sales and underpaid royalties. Many authors suspected fraud but were unable to stop it. They had no legal right to audit printer-publishers.

Authors railed about the unfairness and consoled themselves by focusing on personal satisfaction. They were published. They'd contributed to the culture, left tangible legacies. And if they were lucky, despite piracy and royalty theft, they might make some money.

During the 1820s, two of America's most popular homegrown writers were James Fenimore Cooper, author of *The Last of the Mohicans*, and Washington Irving, author of "Rip Van Winkle" and "The Legend of Sleepy Hollow." They financed their books' manufacture, toured extensively, and sold signed copies after readings. They were also among the first American authors to become popular in England and, eventually, to support themselves as professional writers. In 1825, Cooper earned $6,500 ($150,000 today), and in 1829, Irving made $23,000 ($575,000). Of course, they would have made much more except for you-know-what.

After 1830, small flat-bed presses yielded to steam-driven behemoths that printed from spinning metal cylinders ("plates"). Authors got boxes of books, but printer-publishers retained the plates, which made it easier than ever to reprint without authors' knowledge. When publishers evaded royalty payments, their incomes doubled from 16.5 to 33 percent. Not that every printer-publisher defrauded authors, but given the myriad perils of publishing and authors' inability to audit, the temptation was almost irresistible. In the 1840s, Henry Wadsworth Longfellow, author of the popular poems "Paul Revere's Ride" and "Evangeline," tried to prevent his publisher from reprinting on the sly by repossessing his plates. When the publisher wanted to reprint, Longfellow leased them for 18.5 percent of the retail value of the print run. Of course, Longfellow couldn't verify print runs.

Meanwhile, Noah Webster continued to agitate for perpetual copyright. He eventually won the support of his young cousin, the U.S. senator from Massachusetts Daniel Webster (1782–1852), who engineered the Copyright Act of 1831. It doubled the term to twenty-eight years and allowed one fourteen-year renewal for a total of forty-two.

But the law delivered scant protection. As technological innovations made printing faster, easier, and cheaper, and as the Erie Canal allowed distribution of books beyond the reach of lawsuits, book piracy increased. Some authors became disgusted and quit. The rest huddled under a blanket of resentment and tried to stay warm in a cold, cruel world.

Ironically, for the big names, book piracy had a silver lining. Some readers of pirate editions enjoyed them sufficiently to pay cold cash to see their favorite authors in person. That's how Cooper, Irving, and other top authors made their money: not from royalties, but from touring (much like today's pop stars) and lecturing, with back-of-the-room sales—a combination that thrives to this day.

Speaking gigs took Webster, Irving, and other anti-piracy activists to far-flung towns where fans asked them to autograph pirated copies of their books. Touring authors also discovered pirate editions displayed in local printers' windows. The book thieves were unapologetic: *We made you celebrities. We're the reason you fill lecture halls.* You *should pay* us!

Unimaginably Huge Sales: The Sweet Fruit of Technology

The mid-nineteenth century saw an explosion of consumer spending on books. In 1820, U.S. sales totaled $2.5 million, a generation later $12.5

million. And something previously unimaginable happened. If books caught the public's fancy, the new faster presses could produce enormous quantities quickly, sending sales through the roof. That happened with two of the nineteenth century's biggest books: the first McGuffey Reader (1836) and *Uncle Tom's Cabin* (1852).

Young William McGuffey (1800–1873) taught school on the Ohio frontier, a land almost devoid of books. For reading instruction, students had to bring family Bibles, but few had them. In 1835, a Cincinnati publisher pitched McGuffey on teaching children to read using anthologies of graduated difficulty that incorporated poetry, essays, short stories, and famous oratory. McGuffey saw an opportunity to not only teach reading but also to promote piety, honesty, frugality, patriotism, and hard work.

McGuffey Readers taught nineteenth-century America to read. From 1836 to 1850, an unprecedented seven million copies were sold; during the following two decades, forty million; and from 1870 to 1890, another sixty million. Reprinted in more than five hundred editions, McGuffey Readers are the largest-selling English-language textbooks of all time, with sales of 125 million copies. They're still in print, a favorite of homeschoolers.

Uncle Tom's Cabin, by the New England abolitionist Harriet Beecher Stowe, was an indictment of slavery that humanized Black people, demonized slave owners, and helped spark the Civil War. It was the first American novel to sell a million copies. During its first decade, sales hit seven million. After the Bible, it was the biggest bestseller of the nineteenth century.

Several pulp-fiction authors also generated huge sales. The romance writer Emma Southworth (1819–1899) is forgotten today, but around the Civil War, she transcended the penny-dreadful ghetto and became a big name in trade fiction. Deserted by her husband, Southworth supported her children by writing short stories for newspapers. Her first novel, *Retribution* (1849) didn't sell, but a subsequent title, *The Lost Heiress* (1854) hit big. Over the next twenty-five years, she published sixty novels that sold ten million copies, making her one of the most successful American authors of all time.

Once printing technology made huge sellers possible, they became the holy grail for publishers.

Women Gain a New Occupation: Author

Before the Civil War, other than homemaking, women had few career options beyond teacher, shopkeeper, nurse/midwife, and seamstress/dressmaker. But women loved books and read considerably more than men, especially fiction. The commercial success of Stowe and Southworth paved the way for other women authors, particularly novelists.

No one knows the proportion of nineteenth-century authors who were women. Many wrote under male pseudonyms, and not all emerged from beneath their cloaks. Mary Ann Evans, better known as George Eliot (1819–1880), penned *Silas Marner* (1861). The Brontë sisters, Charlotte (*Jane Eyre*), Emily (*Wuthering Heights*), and Anne (*The Tenant of Wildfell Hall*), launched their literary careers as Currer, Ellis, and Acton Bell. And before Louisa May Alcott published *Little Women*, she wrote under the pen name A. M. Barnard. In 1855, the New York Association of Book Publishers threw a party for the nation's top six hundred authors. Sixty (10 percent) were women.

Since World War II, women have bought two-thirds of all trade books, including around three-quarters of novels. Women continue to read more than men in all categories except history, sports, politics, automotive, military, and biography. But publishing remained male-dominated until the millennium, and even today, as more women populate publishing's top ranks, many women say it still is.

Abolitionists Publish the First Black Authors

Uncle Tom's Cabin awakened white America to the horrors of slavery, but its author was a white New England woman who had no firsthand knowledge of bondage. Abolitionists scoured the North to find escaped slaves who could reinforce the novel's message by telling their stories. It wasn't easy. In the South, it was a crime to teach slaves to read and write, but some enslaved people became literate, and a few escaped to freedom.

The first Black-authored book, *The Interesting Narrative of the Life of Olaudah Equiano*, was published in England. Kidnapped as a child in Africa, Equiano (c. 1745–1797) spent his youth enslaved in Barbados and Virginia. At age twenty, his owner took him to England and sold him to an English Quaker who ran a shipping business and opposed slavery. He taught Equiano to read and paid him for his labor, which allowed him to buy his freedom. In 1789, English abolitionists published his autobiography. His vivid descriptions of the harshness of slavery spurred Parliament to enact the Act for the Abolition of the Slave Trade of 1807.

Frederick Douglass (c. 1818–1895) was born into slavery in rural Maryland. At age six, he was torn from his mother and sold to a family in Baltimore as a domestic servant. White children in the neighborhood taught him to read. In 1838, at age twenty-one, Douglass hid on a train and escaped to freedom, settling in Lynn, Massachusetts. He read William Lloyd Garrison's fiery abolitionist newspaper, the *Liberator*, and heard the man speak. Soon, he was writing for him. Douglass's denunciations of slavery were forceful and eloquent. Garrison arranged publication of his autobiography, *Narrative of the Life of Frederick Douglass, an American Slave, Written by Himself* (1845). Promoted by abolitionists, it became a hit in the United States and Europe.

Solomon Northup (1807–1864?) was born free in upstate New York. In 1841, on a trip to Washington, D.C., he was kidnapped by slavers and spent twelve years in horrific bondage in Louisiana. Eventually, he befriended a white Canadian who got word to his family. New York law provided aid to free Black New Yorkers sold into slavery. The governor of New York intervened. Northup was freed in 1853. Soon after, abolitionists published his memoir, *Twelve Years a Slave* (1853). The 2013 movie adaptation won the Academy Award for Best Picture.

Harriet Jacobs (1813–1897) was born into bondage in North Carolina. Members of her owner's family surreptitiously taught her to read even as Jacobs's enslaver subjected her to relentless sexual harassment. Steadfastly, she refused his advances, and when he threatened to sell her children if she did not submit, she disappeared, hiding in her grandmother's attic, a space so cramped she could not stand up. She spent seven years in her tiny prison, then escaped to the North. Abolitionists published her autobiography, *Incidents in the Life of a Slave Girl, Written by Herself*, in 1861.

Piracy, Burglary, and Arson

As more authors wrote books, more publishers developed creative ways to publish them. Newspapers serialized pirated books, then bootlegged them in their entirety in cheap newsprint editions that cost much less than book publishers' editions. One enthusiastic pirate was the *New World*, a New York–based weekly launched in 1840, whose editor delighted in advertisements that taunted book publishers, especially Harper: "Why pay a dollar for what you can get for 18 cents? We are friends of the people. Our motto: The greatest books to the greatest number."

The Harper brothers denounced *New World*, which fired back, "Ah, ha! . . . The robbers have been robbed. . . . We like to see the pirates made to walk the plank!"

Adding insult to injury, *New World* distributed its cheap pulp editions by mail at ultra-low newspaper rates. Harper complained to the post office, insisting that the newspaper should pay the higher book rate. The post office agreed, forcing *New World* to raise its mail-order price beyond what its market could bear. The newspaper ceased mailing serialized fiction.

But *New World* exacted revenge through its sister weekly, *Brother Jonathan*. (The term was an early personification of the United States, later supplanted by Uncle Sam.) In 1842, *Brother Jonathan*'s editor hired an arsonist to torch Harper's printing plant. The Harpers rebuilt only to be burglarized by a thief who stole the page proofs of Bulwer-Lytton's *The Last of the Barons*. Its advance proof had cost the publisher $1,000 ($30,000 today).

Publishers were both victims of piracy and perpetrators. They railed when their titles were pirated, but most remained unapologetic about their own theft. George Dunlap (1864–1956), cofounder of Grosset & Dunlap (now an imprint of Penguin Random House), justified his house's piracy by saying they were "honourable pirates": "In no case did we ever reprint anything that had not . . . been reprinted indiscriminately by about everyone else in the business."

Meanwhile, in little rooms around the country, thousands of authors dipped their pens into inkwells and searched for the perfect word.

BULWER-LYTTON: "IT WAS A DARK AND STORMY NIGHT . . ."
Edward Bulwer-Lytton is largely forgotten today. But during the 1830s and '40s, he was an English novelist whose pirated books were sensations in America. He coined several familiar phrases: "the almighty dollar," "the great unwashed," and "the pen is mightier than the sword." He also composed one of the most recognizable opening lines in English-language fiction: "It was a dark and stormy night . . ."

That line, from the novel *Paul Clifford* (1830), is but a fragment of the book's actual first sentence: "It was a dark and stormy night; the rain fell in torrents—except at occasional intervals, when it was checked by a violent gust of wind which swept up the streets (for it is in London that our scene lies), rattling along the house-tops, and fiercely agitating the scanty flame of the lamps that struggled against the darkness."

Modern critics consider this terrible writing, so atrocious that in 1982, Scott Rice, an English professor at San José State University in California, inaugurated the Bulwer-Lytton Fiction Contest, which awards annual prizes for the worst first sentences of imaginary novels. The contest attracts thousands of entries each year.

8

The Questionable Dawn of Book Reviewing and "Business Is Business"

If books are the bricks in the foundation of culture, then reviews are the mortar that cements them. Books have value only if they're read and discussed. Reviewers are among books' first readers. Their observations often frame subsequent discussions (if any). But reviewers are subjective, and their reviews may reflect ulterior motives.

Recall that colonial printer-publishers used pseudonyms to extol their own output while deriding that of other printers. Fast-forward to the decades before the Civil War. At that time, few book reviews were published—for two reasons: newspaper and magazine editors viewed books as competition and had no desire to spotlight them, and few readers of the much cheaper periodicals could afford to buy them. Nonetheless, some book reviews appeared, and from all accounts, they were far from trustworthy. In 1832, one essayist pilloried reviewers as "seldom impartial, being guided by prejudices, predilections and venality." One prejudiced reviewer was Mark Twain (1835–1910), who said, "I haven't any right to criticize books, & I don't do it except when I hate them."

Edgar Allan Poe (1809–1849) called book criticism "corrupt": "Intercourse between critic and publisher, as it now almost universally stands, is comprised either in the paying and pocketing of blackmail, as the price of a simple forbearance, or in a direct system of petty and contemptible bribery." That is, publishers bribed reviewers for raves, or reviewers threatened pans unless publishers paid up. The publishing historian John Tebbel called nineteenth-century book reviewing "a corrupt and disgraceful business."

AMERICA'S FIRST BOOK-REVIEW EDITOR WAS A WOMAN
Margaret Fuller (1810–1850) of Cambridge, Massachusetts, was an opinionated newspaper essayist and author of the proto-feminist *Women in the Nineteenth Century* (1845). In 1848, Horace Greeley, editor of the *New-York Tribune*, hired her as the nation's first newspaper book-review editor, making the paper one of the very few to cover books. Tragically, two years later at age forty, Fuller drowned in a boating accident.

Adulation and Bitterness:
Charles Dickens Visits America

Charles Dickens (1812–1870) was the first English-language literary superstar. He lived a "Dickensian" life only briefly. His father spent time in debtors' prison, which forced eleven-year-old Charles to quit school and work for several months from dawn to dusk in a dark, rat-infested boot polish factory under a horrid boss named Fagin, who became the model for the chief pickpocket in *Oliver Twist*. Dickens's factory interlude scarred him and drove him to succeed financially.

Dickens began his writing career as a journalist, then persuaded an English newspaper publisher to serialize his first novel, *The Pickwick Papers*. After a slow start, it took off. Like Noah Webster a generation earlier, Dickens became an "authorpreneur," but with greater techno-logical advantages. Dickens pushed his publisher to use that era's fastest presses to print tens of thousands of copies of the serialized *Pickwick* and distribute them using Britain's fast-growing railroad network. When a book publisher approached him to reprint the novel in one volume, Dickens insisted on two editions, one leather bound on high-quality paper for the affluent, along with a cheap paperback for the hoi polloi. *The Pickwick Papers* became the first mass-culture phenomenon. Amer-ican newspaper and book publishers raced to pirate it and Dickens's subsequent titles, which galled him no end.

In 1842, at age thirty, Dickens arrived in America to rock-star adulation. He minted money at sold-out readings from Boston to Washington, D.C. Audiences greeted him with thunderous applause. He also joined Washington Irving and other American authors in endorsing a petition urging Congress to enact an international copyright treaty to stop trans-atlantic book piracy. This infuriated the buccaneers who ran America's newspapers. Editorials called him a prissy ingrate. *We made you famous!* In Washington, Congress rebuffed the international copyright petition. Returning home richer but bitter, Dickens avenged himself in *Martin Chuzzlewit* by sending his protagonist to America to seek his fortune, only to encounter vicious thieves and almost perish of malaria in a swampy settlement called Eden.

Dickens's fury abated somewhat when the Harper brothers offered to buy proofs for $30,000 ($900,000 today). Other publishers also bought Dickens's galleys, touting their payments as proof they'd renounced piracy. But all his life Dickens believed he'd been fleeced.

HARPER'S: BOOK PUBLISHERS LAUNCH MAGAZINES

The Harper brothers wanted free publicity for their new books. They offered magazine publishers free excerpts of about-to-be-published titles ("first serial rights"), hoping they would entice readers to buy. To the Harpers, this was a win-win. Their titles got free publicity, while magazine publishers got free editorial content. But magazine publishers considered books competition and weren't interested.

In 1850, Harper launched its own magazine, *Harper's New Monthly*, with a run of 7,500 copies. Three years later, circulation topped 130,000. The magazine published first serials and general-interest material.

Not to be outdone, in 1857, Ticknor & Fields acquired the *Atlantic Monthly*. Other book publishers also launched magazines: *Putnam's Monthly*, *Scribner's Monthly*, and *Lippincott's Magazine*. But by 1900, only *Harper's* and the *Atlantic* remained. Both survive today, but neither is owned by book publishers.

"Courtesy Is Courtesy, but Business Is Business"

In 1841, G. P. Putnam arrived in London as pirate in chief for Wiley & Putnam and shipped hundreds of titles to New York for unauthorized reprinting. During his six years in England, Putman socialized with British publishers, who must have watched him as closely as relatives supervising a kleptomaniac cousin at the family reunion.

To irritate Putnam, English publishers boasted about pirating *American* titles, among them *Uncle Tom's Cabin*, whose bootleg English editions sold 1.5 million copies. Surprised that the snooty Brits had any interest in Yankee books, Putnam documented 382 reverse-pirated works. As the years passed and the American book business grew, so did English piracy—and pirated American titles often sold better in England than at home.

In 1847, Putnam returned to New York convinced book piracy was a mistake—not wrong, mind you, but bad for business. He argued that exploding English theft of American titles cost American publishers more than pirated English books earned them. Putnam became the first American publisher to renounce piracy. He insisted that Wiley & Putnam negotiate contracts with foreign authors and pay standard royalties (which authors could not audit).

In 1848, Putnam signed Fredrika Bremer (1801–1865), a big-name Swedish novelist, and announced the contract in the trade press, invoking courtesy of the trade to prevent piracy. But seconds after Wiley & Putnam released Bremer's titles, Harper pirated them.

In 1849, Bremer visited New York. Putnam escorted her to Harper, demanding that the brothers stop pirating her and honor courtesy of the trade. "Courtesy is courtesy," Fletcher Harper replied, "but business is business."

During the Civil War, the South used book piracy to alienate England from the North. In 1861, the Confederacy offered England an attractive copyright treaty. The South's one significant publisher, West & Johnston of Richmond, Virginia, signed contracts with several English authors, explaining that the Brits had been "robbed, by Yankee swindlers," and insisting that "the disgraceful proceeding is no part of Southern practice."

Tebbel: "In fairness . . . some [American] publishers did pay royalties to some foreign authors in some instances, and official company histories have been quick to point this out in defending the ethics of the founders. But the fact is that no [U.S.] publisher was wholly guiltless in this respect . . . and about all one can say of the prevailing ethical standards is that the best publishers were better than the worst."

The Sun Sets on the First Book Business

American authors self-published for two hundred years, from the colonial era through the late nineteenth century. Then, from around 1870 to World War I, the model flipped. Publishers began hiring authors and paying for book production—thanks to huge, new, lightning-fast presses that reduced per-copy print costs lower than ever. Industrial printing launched the second book business.

Spurring this transition was readers' insatiable appetite for cheap books. Increasingly literate Americans loved to turn pages, but books remained beyond the means of many. Industrial printing changed that. It allowed fewer people than ever to produce many more copies of more books faster than ever at lower unit cost.

Today's publishing people call the second book business "traditional" publishing. Actually, in the centuries since Gutenberg, publishers paid production costs for only around eighty years, from World War I through the millennium.

Since 2000, the book business has bifurcated. Publishers continue to pay to print the big names and second-tier authors who win awards or ascend to prominence in their niches. But these days, the vast majority of authors pay to publish, just as Thoreau and Washington Irving did.

From this perspective, the second book business is hardly "traditional," but a brief eight-decade detour from the long and winding six-century road of most authors financing publication of their work. Still, the second book business lasted five generations, and for the favored few authors, it still endures. "Traditional publishing" is a misnomer, but it continues to define how many people conceive of book publishing.

Part II

The Second Book Business

Industrial Publishing

From World War I to 2000

9

Publishing Industrializes and Carnegie Builds 1,689 Libraries

The second book business—publishers hiring authors—was a direct result of the industrial revolution, the most fundamental change in civilization since the invention of agriculture (c. 8000 BCE). Beginning in England around 1760, the industrial revolution involved a giant technological leap. Instead of streams producing power by turning waterwheels, coal-fired engines produced steam and much more power. This enabled construction of enormous new machines on a scale previously unimagined: steamships, locomotives, mechanized factories, and enormous printing presses.

America's industrial revolution lagged fifty years behind England's, but it germinated in 1830, when Peter Cooper's Tom Thumb, the first American-made steam locomotive, ran thirteen miles from Baltimore to Ellicott's Mills, Maryland (now Ellicott City).

Wooden printing presses were too fragile to be powered by steam. Starting in the 1770s, innovators replaced some wood members with iron. In 1803, the English inventor Charles Stanhope (1753–1816) constructed the first all-iron press. It not only accommodated steam power but also sharpened printing. By 1811, Stanhope presses were being manufactured in the United States.

During the decade before the Civil War, small steam-powered presses boosted print speeds from five hundred sheets an hour to five thousand.

After the war, behemoth industrialized presses printed an astounding twenty thousand pages an hour—and a few people could produce an avalanche of books faster and cheaper than ever, reducing books' unit cost considerably.

But to achieve this economy of scale, printer-publishers had to invest tons of money to acquire the new faster presses and then print many more copies per title. This required a mountain of cash up front—more paper, ink, warehousing, and increasingly skilled pressmen. This substantially increased printer-publishers' costs and risk. Frequently, their bets did not pay off. Presses broke down. Warehouses burned or flooded. Books were lost to shipping misfortunes. Or printer-publishers guessed wrong about sales, leaving them with warehouses of books nobody wanted. Many printer-publishers went bankrupt or stopped printing books.

In Ben Franklin's day, authors could recoup the cost of hiring printers by selling around a hundred copies. But after the Civil War, the industrialization of publishing raised the break-even figure to five hundred. Few part-time authors could afford to finance that many, let alone shoulder the cost and increasing hassle of distributing books to distant booksellers. Working under contract to publishers who handled printing, warehousing, and distribution looked like a better bet.

Industrialization finalized the separation of printing from publishing. Most publishers sold their printing plants and began contracting with independent printers. Meanwhile, as titles proliferated and print runs increased, title acquisition, warehousing, distribution, sales, and promotion became more complex and competitive. In addition, businesses adopted new tools: the telegraph (invented in 1837 and commercialized by the Civil War), typewriters (1873), and telephones (1876).

Industrialization transformed distribution of all products, including books. Canals proliferated, and steam-powered vessels cut the cost of shipping. The nation's rail system expanded. From 1840 to 1870, American track mileage soared from 3,300 to 50,000. But again, while unit shipping costs declined, total distribution costs rose. Profit depended on sending more copies of more titles to more destinations farther away from where they were printed.

A new niche developed: book wholesaling. Regional wholesalers established warehouses beyond the Appalachians and coordinated distribution throughout their territories. But wholesaling was a two-edged sword. Publishers benefited by shipping in bulk to wholesalers' warehouses and letting them cover the growing number of booksellers throughout their regions. But wholesalers' slice of the pie pinched publishers' margins. Worse, while wholesalers were happy to stock every title, they often took sixty days or ninety or longer to pay—if they paid at all. Meanwhile, printers demanded payment in thirty days. The disparity caused cash-flow nightmares that bankrupted many publishers.

Some authors clung to the old entrepreneurial model, but most preferred the solitary pursuit of the bon mot, with perhaps some lecturing, to the new, more competitive, more capital-intensive, bare-knuckle book business. From 1870 to World War I, as printing and publishing diverged, most authors stopped hiring printers and signed up with the growing number of publishers who hired authors. The book business started to revolve around the new publishers, becoming publisher-centric.

Authors had mixed feelings about this change. If they penned the next *Uncle Tom's Cabin*, the second book business could make them rich. But big books were rare. Meanwhile, like farmers who became factory workers, industrial publishing transformed the large majority of authors from independent entrepreneurs into tiny cogs in an impersonal machine.

Publishers felt equally ambivalent. Back in the good old days, authors paid to print, and printer-publishers profited from every title—usually not much, but every book finished in the black. In the second book business, publishers walked a tightrope. If books took off, they bought mansions. But very few books did. Meanwhile, huge printing and shipping bills arrived daily. Creditors clamored for payment.

No local market could absorb the deluge of titles being released, not even New York City, whose population swelled to one million in 1875. Sales to distant markets became increasingly key to profitability. But despite preferential postal rates, the mail was expensive. Steamships were affordable, but many destinations were unreachable by water. Railroad freight charges were exorbitant. And piracy continued unabated.

Meanwhile, the nation's bookshops lacked the shelf space to stock all the titles industrial presses produced. For the first time, booksellers began *declining* some new releases, and publishers became more selective about title acquisition. Many authors opened letters saying: *Alas, your manuscript does not meet our current needs.*

Courtesy of the Trade Bites the Dust

In 1864, Henry Houghton purchased proofs of a Dickens novel and hoped to prevent piracy by advertising a courtesy-of-the-trade claim. When another publisher pirated the book, Houghton sued, arguing that courtesy of the trade reflected "gentlemanly conduct, and a feeling among respectable [publishers] that one ought not to interfere with the business of another."

The judge scoffed. Publishers had never adhered to the practice, and even if they had, no gentleman's agreement carried the force of law. With that decision, courtesy of the trade evaporated.

Few readers were aware of book piracy, and those who knew hardly cared. They just wanted more books cheaper. As the second book business matured, competition turned ferocious, and any publisher who hoped to stay afloat had no choice but to pirate. One justified it, saying, "We don't steal for ourselves; we steal for the benefit of the public."

Subscription Book Sales Boom

Some eighteenth-century printers tried the subscription model without much success. But after the Civil War, it became a winner, thanks to improved transportation and shipping to a more widely dispersed population. When it worked, subscription publishing offered a sweet deal. Buyers ordered books *before* they were printed, eliminating press-run guesswork. And they bought directly from publishers, not middlemen. Eliminating wholesalers' and booksellers' cuts paid for advertising and postage, while still earning publishers healthy profits.

Books by subscription worked marvelously for Americans who lived far from bookshops. The best way to sell books had always been word of mouth, readers touting titles to friends or, in current parlance, "social networking." Publishers thought, *Let's offer farm folks commissions to talk up subscriptions to their neighbors.*

In 1870, a Hartford, Connecticut, publisher advertised for subscription agents in rural newspapers: "The sale of our works is an honorable and praiseworthy employment, and is particularly adapted to disabled

[Civil War] Soldiers, aged and other Clergymen having leisure hours, Teachers and Students during vacations, &c."

Subscription publishers signed up more than ten thousand agents, mostly farm women who combined part-time bookselling with social calls. From 1870 to 1900, subscription agents moved 1.4 million copies annually, grossed $5 million a year, and accounted for two-thirds of trade book sales. (Bookshops claimed one-quarter of sales, book fairs and specialty shops the rest.)

But the subscription model was perilous. Instead of printing a few hundred catalogues for bookshops, publishers had to print thousands, one per agent. If publishers required agents to pay for books up front, sales suffered. But if publishers offered credit, they might never collect. Consequently, many subscription publishers failed.

FROM STEEL TO BOOKS: CARNEGIE LIBRARIES

Free, tax-supported public libraries were rare until the 1880s, when upper-crust women's organizations embraced the Gilded Age notion that books, and therefore libraries, civilized the unruly masses. Ladies' clubs lobbied for public libraries—vocally supported by the American Library Association, founded in 1876. Their efforts, combined with noblesse oblige, inspired steel-magnate-turned-philanthropist Andrew Carnegie (1835-1919) to finance the construction of 1,689 public library buildings in major cities and small towns, including the one eight blocks from my home. By 1900, Carnegie libraries accounted for half the nation's public libraries.

The new libraries needed books, and publishers reaped a bonanza:

Year	U.S population	Public libraries	Books held	One library book for every...
1876	46 million	2,500	12 million	3.8 Americans
1900	76 million	5,000	40 million	1.9

During the final quarter of the nineteenth century, America's population increased 40 percent, but thanks to Carnegie, the number of public libraries doubled and their holdings more than tripled. Publishers rejoiced.

10

Publishers and Authors Undeterred by "Too Many Books"

A generation after the Civil War, readers were more numerous than books, so almost every title sold. Industrial publishing changed that. Suddenly, books were plentiful and increasingly affordable. Starting around 1875, publishers began voicing a novel complaint. There were "too many" books.

Several factors contributed to the perceived glut:

More new releases. By 1870, American publishers numbered 1,200, enough to support a trade magazine, *Publishers Weekly* (*PW*), which debuted in 1872. In 1880, the journal began tracking American book production:

Year	U.S. population	Book releases	One release for every ...
1880	50 million	2,700	18,519 Americans
1914	99 million	12,010	8,243

Over those thirty-five years, the population almost doubled, but book releases more than quadrupled—for the first time, surpassing England.

Average print runs also rose from 1,000 in 1885 to 1,500 in 1914. *PW* observed that publishers were "issuing thousands of books where a generation ago American presses produced only hundreds." In 1894, *Lippincott's Magazine* observed: "Literature (or what aims to be such) is overdone; there is too much of it."

Bigger backlists. By the 1880s, established publishers, including Harper, Lippincott, and Little, Brown, had amassed substantial "backlists," old titles that sold modestly but steadily year after year. When sales of new releases ("front lists") were disappointing, backlist sales could mean the difference between solvency and bankruptcy. But growing backlists also competed with front lists, which hurt sales of new releases.

Remainders. As unit costs declined and publishers released more copies of more books, some could hardly be given away. Unsold books ("remainders") became a costly problem.

The issue was not returns from booksellers. Until the 1930s, publishers didn't accept them. The problem was the rising number of books that never left publishers' warehouses. In 1894, *PW* opined: "The tendency of modern publishing has been toward over-production without regard to capacity for consumption." And in 1900, the magazine sniffed: "Books are becoming what newspapers and magazines have always been—ephemeral."

Rather than incinerate surplus copies, publishers doubled down on book fairs, selling remainders at huge discounts. In 1867, when hardcover books sold for one to two dollars, a New York book fair offered them for an average of just thirty-three cents—and in eight days sold nine hundred thousand. Of course, like their predecessors, booksellers protested bitterly against book fairs but could do nothing to stop them.

Publishers also tried vending machines. In 1888, the first coin-operated sales devices offered gumballs on New York City train platforms. Soon after, publishers deployed vending machines that offered five-cent excerpts that included coupons for discounts on the books. Booksellers loved this idea. Readers redeemed the coupons at their stores. But vending machine sales did not justify publishers' investment, and they dropped the idea.

In 1925, the *Atlantic Monthly* carried an article by "a New York publisher" rumored to be George P. Brett (1893–1984), president of Macmillan, who said the industry's output of nine thousand titles a year could easily be reduced to 7,000 without any loss to the reading public. But no publisher cut titles or reduced print runs because of too many books. They felt free to release all the titles they wished, while arguing that *everyone else* should reduce output—especially the scoundrels who published pulp fiction.

Of course, even in the best of times, businesspeople complain. While publishers and *PW* griped about too many books, in 1908, *Munsey's Magazine* declared the period "a golden harvest" for publishers with plenty of titles to suit every taste and budget, new Carnegie libraries buying books by the trainload, and labor unions winning higher wages and shorter workweeks, giving more people more money to buy books and more time to read them.

TOO MANY BOOKS? THEN AND NOW

Year	U.S population	New Releases	One new title for every...
1880	50 million	2,700	18,519 people
2021	332 million	2,700,000	123 people

In my humble opinion, there can never be too many books, just too few readers with too little time to read.

The New Publishers:
Scribner, Holt, Doubleday, and Knopf

The years from 1870 through World War I were anything but golden. Many publishers and booksellers folded. But publishing looked sufficiently lucrative and prestigious to attract many new booklovers—and for the first time, few started as printers.

• Charles Scribner (1821–1871), an upper-crust New Yorker, graduated from Princeton University in 1840 and became a partner in a small publisher, Baker & Scribner. After his death, his sons took over, renaming the house Charles Scribner's Sons. Today it's an imprint of Simon & Schuster.

• Henry Holt (1840–1926), son of a Maryland oysterman, attended Yale intending to study law. But a classmate introduced him to George Palmer Putnam, who hooked him on publishing. In 1866, he became a partner in Leypoldt & Holt. The house became Henry Holt & Company in 1873. For fifty years, Holt was a towering figure in publishing. Today, Holt is an imprint of Macmillan.

• Frank Doubleday (1862–1934) grew up in Brooklyn and, at age twelve, bought a small used printing press for fifteen dollars, producing what he called "the worst visiting [greeting] cards the world has ever seen." For eighteen years, Doubleday worked for Charles Scribner. In 1900, he founded Doubleday, Page & Company, which became Doubleday & Company in 1946. Today, it's an imprint of Penguin Random House.

• Alfred A. Knopf (1892–1984) graduated from Columbia University in 1912 and worked for Doubleday. In 1915, he founded the house bearing his name. Today, it's an imprint of Penguin Random House.

By World War I, the book business had largely industrialized. But compared with the nation's manufacturing giants, publishing houses remained small and entrepreneurial, averaging just two dozen employees.

Finally, International Copyright

After Dickens lobbied Congress in favor of international copyright, English diplomats needled the U.S. State Department about book piracy. In 1852, they found a sympathetic ear in Edward Everett (1794–1865), President Millard Fillmore's secretary of state, who pledged to pursue a treaty—if the idea flew with printers, publishers, and booksellers. It didn't. *It will raise book prices! It's un-American!*

But Everett persevered, and in 1853, with the help of G. P. Putnam and Charles Scribner, he drafted a treaty. Congress killed it. Thus began forty years of successive administrations sending copyright treaties to Congress and the paper-printer-publisher-bookseller lobby scuttling them.

In 1867, Dickens returned to America for another triumphant tour. This time, he negotiated an exclusive contract with Ticknor & Fields that finally granted his wish: a 10 percent royalty on U.S. sales. Harper, Houghton, and Lippincott denounced the deal and continued to pirate his books. Dickens never knew if he actually benefited from the arrangement; he couldn't audit Ticknor & Fields. In 1878, T&F failed. Houghton Mifflin bought its name and backlist, retaining it as an imprint well into the twentieth century. Today Houghton Mifflin is owned by Veritas Capital, a private equity firm.

Meanwhile, American authors' laments over English piracy gained traction in Congress.

• Nathaniel Hawthorne: "Of the ten works I have written, seven have been republished in England. I received in all $275 for works which had a circulation of over one hundred thousand."

• Henry Wadsworth Longfellow: "I have had twenty-two publishers in England and Scotland, and only four of them ever took the slightest notice of my existence, even so far as to send me a copy."

• And Mark Twain implored Congress to make book piracy punishable by imprisonment "like any other stealing."

Prominent academics also touted international copyright. In 1885, the Columbia University professor Brander Matthews (1852–1929) surveyed four English publishers' catalogues and documented the proportion of pirated American titles: 40 to 89 percent.

Nonetheless, American publishers fought international copyright. They wanted to continue pirating English books. Eventually, *Publishers Weekly* editorialized in favor, bravely accusing its advertising base, notably Harper, of intransigence. And as English publishers sold increasing numbers of pirated American titles, U.S. publishers realized the centuries-old practice was a loser.

In 1875, Joseph Harper tabulated what his house had spent on advance sheets: $250,000 ($5.4 million today). He also estimated Harper's losses to English piracy. His figures made a strong case for international copyright.

In 1880, President Rutherford Hayes invited prominent American publishers and authors to draft a treaty with England. *Publishers Weekly* surveyed fifty-five publishers. Only three (5 percent) were opposed.

But Congress was a different story. Paper and printing moguls lobbied hard against any treaty, fearing it would raise book prices and hurt business. Southerners called the proposed treaty a Yankee plot to gouge book buyers. And westerners recoiled from any infringement of their God-given right to pirate whatever they wanted. Despite the howling, in 1891, the treaty passed, granting copyright protection in the United States to all books by all authors of all nations published after that year.

Of course, the devil was in the details. The treaty denied protection to works deemed libelous, immoral, or blasphemous. As a result, many books continued to be pirated with impunity: those criticizing living persons, depicting anything sexual, or taking the Lord's name in vain— even books whose characters exclaimed, "Oh my God."

A few prominent authors on both sides of the Atlantic earned substantial income from foreign rights and royalties, but for the vast majority of book writers, international copyright produced little if any benefit. As opponents predicted, American publishers raised prices, prompting the American Library Association's Committee on Book Buying to denounce them for "fattening their purses at the public's expense."

More Black Authors Get Published

Despite the outcome of the Civil War, through World War II, the publishing industry was entirely populated by white people, most of whom were not interested in writers who were immigrants or people of color. But despite major barriers to entry, during the late nineteenth and early twentieth centuries, some immigrants and Black writers worked their way into print, and some became part of the American literary canon:

•Charles W. Chesnutt (1858–1932) was born in Ohio to racially mixed free people of color. He could pass for white but always identified as Black. He worked as a teacher, then became a lawyer, and had short stories published in the *Atlantic Monthly*. Encouraged by the magazine's editors, he wrote several novels, including *The Marrow of Tradition* (1901), a fictionalized account of the 1898 white supremacist pogrom that killed more than two hundred Black people in Wilmington, North Carolina.

• W. E. B. Du Bois (1868–1963) grew up in relatively racially tolerant Great Barrington, Massachusetts. He was the first Black American to earn a PhD (from Harvard). He became a professor of history, sociology, and economics at Atlanta University and was a founder of the National Association for the Advancement of Colored People. His books include *The Souls of Black Folk* (1903), a seminal work on Black history and sociology now considered a cornerstone of African American literature.

• Booker T. Washington (1856–1915) was born into slavery in Virginia. After emancipation, he worked his way through a historically Black college there, Hampton Normal and Agricultural Institute (now Hampton University). He was a founder and the longtime head of the Tuskegee Normal and Industrial Institute (now Tuskegee University) in Alabama and spent his long career as an educator, author, orator, spokesman for Black Americans, and adviser to several U.S. presidents. His best-known book is his autobiography, *Up from Slavery* (1901).

• James Weldon Johnson (1871–1938) grew up in Florida and moved to New York during the Great Migration. In 1901, he wrote a poem that was later set to music, "Lift Every Voice and Sing," now widely considered the Black national anthem. His best-known book is the novel *The Autobiography of an Ex-Colored Man* (1912), which traces the life of a mixed-race, light-skinned Georgia man who witnesses a lynching and decides to pass for white.

• Nella Larsen (1891–1964) grew up in Chicago in a mixed-race family. She attended historically Black Fish University in Nashville, then nursing school. She became the head nurse at the Tuskegee Institute. During the 1920s, she left nursing to become a librarian in New York City, which led to a literary career. Her loosely autobiographical novel, *Quicksand* (1928), tells the story of a mixed-race woman who feels torn between white and Black society.

• Zora Neale Hurston (1891–1960) was born in Alabama and grew up in Florida in a sharecropping family. She attended historically Black Howard University in Washington, D.C., and Barnard College in New York, where she was involved in anthropological research on the Black South. While living in New York, she befriended many writers and artists involved in the Harlem Renaissance, the Black cultural flowering of the 1920s and '30s. They encouraged her writing. Her books include *Their Eyes Were Watching God* (1937), a harrowing novel that follows a sexually abused Black Florida woman who is accused of murder.

• Langston Hughes (1901–1967) was born in Missouri. He attended high school in Cleveland, Ohio, and college at Columbia University. His articles in the NAACP magazine the *Crisis* brought him to the attention of publishers. Hughes was a leader of the Harlem Renaissance, a poet, an essayist, and a journalist. His collection of short stories, *The Ways of White Folks* (1934), is a meditation on race relations.

• Richard Wright (1908–1960) grew up poor near Natchez, Mississippi, and spent part of his youth in an orphanage. At age seventeen, he landed in Memphis, Tennessee, eager to read books, but the public library did not lend to Black people. Wright borrowed a white friend's library card and wrote a note saying he was picking up books for his buddy. The ruse worked. In 1927, Wright moved to Chicago and worked as a postal clerk. His articles for several leftist magazines brought him to the attention of publishers. His two best-known books are *Native Son* (1940) and

Black Boy (1945). The former is a novel about an impoverished Black youth living on the South Side of Chicago in the 1930s. The latter is a memoir of Wright's youth in the South.

= 11 =

From "The Doom of Books" to Department Stores, with Authors as Supplicants in the "Gentlemanly" Book Business

The high-speed presses that slashed book-printing costs did the same for newspapers and magazines. By the 1880s, periodicals had become so numerous, popular, and cheap that book publishers felt threatened. In 1887, publishers released a record 4,437 new titles, but Henry Holt was among the first to suggest the death of books "due to the great development of newspapers and periodicals. Many a man who used to read a book of some kind on Sunday now takes all his time to read his Sunday paper[, which] contains as much reading matter as an average novel, and it can be had for five cents, where the book costs . . . a dollar. . . . In view of this, then, begins to come up the question: 'Will the coming man read books?'"

Two years later, with 88 percent of Americans literate and Carnegie libraries disseminating more books more widely than ever, new releases increased to 4,484, and optimists proclaimed a golden age for literature. But that same year, 1894, a *Scribner's* headline blared, "The Doom of Books; or, What the Phonograph Will Do." The article predicted that Edison's new talking machine would destroy both books and reading as libraries jettisoned print and became little more than record collections. (What would they have thought of Audible?)

This was just the first of many erroneous predictions of the imminent demise of books. Sadly many of those who feel most invested in reading and have gained the most from it (for example, Henry Holt) have shown the least faith in it. The fact is reading is resilient. Not everyone reads, but a substantial portion of the population *loves* to read, no matter what other media are available.

Which raises a question: Where do they obtain their books?

Department Stores Become Booksellers

In 1858, the New York men's clothier Rowland Hussey Macy (1822–1877) expanded into women's clothing and housewares, making R. H. Macy & Company America's first department store. In 1869, hoping for cachet to attract the carriage trade, Macy added a few leather-bound books.

In 1877, a Philadelphia men's clothier, Wanamaker's, became the nation's second department store and also offered books—ten titles at the stationery counter. They sold well. Wanamaker's launched a stand-alone book department, and Macy's quickly followed. By the 1880s, other department stores also offered books, including Hudson's in Detroit and Montgomery Ward in Chicago. Soon, department stores were a major force in bookselling. Publishers rejoiced: *More outlets!* But the guardians of culture recoiled: *Selling books next to underwear degrades literature.* Nonetheless, by the early twentieth century, department stores accounted for one-third of trade sales, and after the Depression, half (more than Amazon's current market share).

Department stores dominated bookselling for more than sixty years, from the late nineteenth century until the late 1950s. Their hegemony is largely forgotten today, but it paved the way for chain booksellers in the late twentieth century and Amazon in the twenty-first.

Bookshops ordered a few copies of new titles, but department stores ordered dozens, sometimes hundreds. Larger orders brought bigger wholesale discounts from publishers, which Macy's et al. rolled into retail discounts. They sold books below list at prices independent booksellers could not match and boosted their market share at the indies' expense. In 1900, Macy's cut book prices from one dollar to seventy-nine cents, then sixty-nine, and finally fifty-nine. Macy's insisted the goal was to attract new customers, not kill independents, but scores of indies failed.

Independent booksellers considered wholesale and retail discounting monopolistic and predatory. In 1884, a *PW* writer called the booksellers demoralized. According to publishing historian Tebbel, for booksellers "it was an impossible situation." This siege mentality was nothing new. A century earlier, the independents had railed against book fairs. Now it was department stores, and subsequently, chain booksellers (Barnes & Noble et al.), and today Amazon. It's always tough being David in a world of Goliaths.

Publishers gave lip service to the indies' plight but continued to favor department stores. *PW* supported publishers' favoritism. In 1880, the magazine editorialized, "The trouble is that the [independent] bookseller simply puts the book on his counter and lets him buy who will. That is not the way to *sell* books." But *PW* offered no marketing advice.

In 1900, independent booksellers organized the American Booksellers Association (ABA) to combat wholesale and retail discounting. But department store discounting continued unabated. For sixty years, from the 1890s through the 1950s, department stores grew, added new locations, and left a trail of failed independent booksellers in their wake. Some authors rallied around the indies, but the industry trend was clear: department stores were the princes; indie booksellers, the peasants.

Just Write—Then Get Out of the Way

And what of authors? During the first book business, the writing was often the easy part. The real challenges involved mustering the capital to manufacture one's books and then finding the money and entrepreneurial zeal to market them despite daunting distribution hurdles and rampant piracy.

The second book business arrived singing a tune that was music to authors' ears: *Just write.* Publishers would handle everything else. Legions of ambitious readers set their sights on becoming authors.

Their numbers turned the emerging business model into a cotillion where the myriad authors hoped that the comparatively few publishers might ask them to dance. As the second book business matured, these relatively few publishers dictated terms, and the overwhelming majority of authors and aspiring authors had little leverage. They became supplicants begging for contracts.

Publishers used their new clout to squeeze authors. Gone were the days when Longfellow licensed his plates for 18.5 percent. As the second book business gelled, publishers retained plates—and charged non-big names to make them. Around 1900, Charles Scribner wrote one author, "We are not sufficiently sure of its commercial success to justify us in running the entire risk of the manufacture of the book. Our proposal therefore is that you bear the expense of making the plates." (It was not until after World War I that the major publishers began underwriting publication costs for most authors.)

During the first book business, authors financed their books but retained control (except for piracy). Now the majority of authors still paid to publish but lost all power. Publishers signed no contracts and dictated everything: press runs, promotion, publicity, and duration in print, communicating with authors infrequently, rarely sending royalty statements let alone checks, and when checks arrived, quite often they wouldn't buy a stick of Wrigley's chewing gum (introduced in 1892). In an 1886 editorial, *Publishers Weekly* crystallized the change: "The publisher has usually in bargaining with the author the advantage . . . the author seeks him rather than he the author."

When authors complained, publishers listed the challenges they faced: too many books, exorbitant press costs, greedy printers, the book distribution meat grinder, feckless booksellers, wholesalers who never paid, and mountains of remainders. All true. Publishers also used their myriad complaints to justify rejecting an increasing proportion of man- uscripts. In 1873, Horace Scudder (1838–1902), editor of the *Atlantic Monthly*, editorialized: "When one sees the load which every book has to bear of expense before [breaking even], one is tempted to say—Go back, poor little book, into the brain of your author, and venture not into this groaning world."

Publishers and *Publishers Weekly* beat the drum of too many books. The message to authors was clear and stark: *We don't need you. We're drowning under more titles than we can sell. If we deign to publish you, we're doing you an enormous favor. Never forget it.*

From 1870 through World War I, publishers paid production costs for the big names, while most authors continued to finance their books' publication as they had since colonial times. Their publishers were book releasers for hire, or publishing services companies (PSCs). But unlike colonial printers, PSCs offered more than just book manufacture. Services included warehousing, sales, distribution, accounting, and disposal of remainders, as publishers pumped both types of books—publisher-financed and author-financed—through the same pipeline.

Early twentieth-century authors who paid to publish chafed at the arrangement, but PSCs offered them a novel benefit: protection from the developing bias against self- or "vanity" publishing. As the author-centric first book business yielded to the publisher-centric second, the new publishers bolstered their growing hegemony by stigmatizing the previous model. Self-publishing became toxic. Publishers and pundits derided it as the last refuge of losers who couldn't attract "real" publishers. But authors who signed PSC contracts acquired PR cover. Only they and their publishers knew who paid whom, so they could tell their friends, *Great news! Harper [or whoever] is publishing my book.* The PSC model faded in the 1920s as the majors eventually paid all authors for manuscripts (usually not much) and assumed books' manufacturing costs. A century later, the third book business has resurrected the PSC model (see Part III).

This period also marked the birth of the industry axiom that 70 percent of new titles lose money, 20 percent break even (that is, make or lose less than $1,000), and only 10 percent soar. The implication was unmistakable. If only one book in ten made cash registers ring, then publishers were, indeed, doing nine out of ten authors a big favor. In addition to insisting that authors underwrite some or all publication costs, many publishers excluded from royalties the first one thousand copies to reimburse their overhead.

Meanwhile, literacy increased, more Carnegie libraries opened, and industrialization raised the standard of living, giving more Americans more income to buy more books. Sales grew steadily. The second book business made some publishers—many of whose names we still recognize—wealthy. But they denied it. In 1894, *Lippincott's Magazine* (owned by the book publisher) claimed, "Most books get printed ... at the author's expense and risk. This is fair, because the publishers ought not to bear all the losses. Very few books are producers of wealth." When authors complained, *PW* rose to the defense of its advertisers, in 1886 editorializing, "The element of risk in the book business is, in fact, very large; if the author complains . . . he can get over the difficulty by taking the risk himself."

In 1896, some did, founding the Associated Authors Publishing Company. They raised $50,000 by selling 2,500 shares to writers at twenty dollars each. But the founders were more idealistic than entrepreneurial. The company released a few titles, then went bankrupt.

John Tebbel noted that a "characteristic of American book publishing was its early image as a 'gentleman's business,' although the men who founded these houses . . . had to soil their hands in the marketplace as much as anyone. Nevertheless, there was something genteel about publishing in the public mind."

How did the bare-knuckle book business gain such an enduring reputation for gentility? Gilded Age sensibilities. The late nineteenth-century cultural elite considered books elevated above other manufactured goods. They extended the distinction to those who produced them. Who would populate such a noble enterprise? Greedy bastards? Oh no. *Gentlemen.* To this day, much of the public and many authors still believe that, compared with other industries, book publishing is better.

WAS THE 70-20-10 STATISTIC TRUE?

The idea that 70 percent of books lose money, 20 percent break even, and only 10 percent make big bucks was a hallmark of twentieth-century publishing lore. Was it true?

Publishers have never revealed profit-loss statements by title, but my agent's experience provides some insight. By 2000, she had represented around one thousand titles. Her breakdown was around 60-20-20—that is, 60 percent of her authors' books did not recoup their advances ("earn out"), 20 percent broke even, and 20 percent made good money. More were profitable than the publishers' breakdown suggests.

None of my four novels made a nickel. Of my fourteen nonfiction titles, six lost money, three broke even, and six produced income ranging from modest to renovate-the-kitchen. In total, that's a breakdown of 53-16-31. Maybe I was lucky. Or perhaps the publishers' statistic was just another myth.

=== 12 ===

Authors Flock to Agents as Editing Becomes Formalized and Covers Become Billboards

It wasn't until the 1890s that authors attempted to form trade organizations, but none lasted long. Perhaps—as publishers alleged—authors were too individualistic to unite for their common good. Then in 1912, authors formed the Authors League of America, later rechristened the Authors Guild. The new organization itemized its members' demands:

- Written contracts
- Consultation on editorial changes
- Projected publication dates
- Publication by the projected dates
- Periodic royalty statements
- No royalty exclusions for the first one thousand copies
- Complimentary author copies
- Discounts for author purchases
- Revenue sharing from foreign rights sales or magazine and newspaper excerpts
- Notification of books being taken out of print
- Option to buy out-of-print stock at the same discount publishers offered remainder jobbers

In 1916, the Authors Guild produced a model contract and royalty statement and lobbied publishers to adopt them both. Initially, publishers scoffed, but eventually, the Guild won most of its demands by rallying celebrity authors to its cause and with the help of new players in the industry: literary agents.

Agents: From "Parasites" to Inevitable

The first literary agent was A. P. Watt (1834–1914), an Edinburgh bookseller who moved to London and worked for a publisher until the company failed. In 1875, a friend asked him to market his stories, which Watt did as a favor. But Watt saw opportunity. Soon he was charging 10 percent of the gross to represent Rudyard Kipling, Thomas Hardy, and Arthur Conan Doyle, among others. Watt's 10 percent commission remained standard until the 1980s, when agents bumped it to 15 percent.

The first American agent was the Bostonian Paul Reynolds (1864–1944). In 1891, after the international copyright treaty, he sold English rights to American publishers. In 1895, he began representing American authors.

The arrival of literary agents signaled three developments:

• Publishing had become sufficiently lucrative for agents to earn decent livings from just 10 percent of client royalties.

• Authors were sick of having no leverage and craved advocates.

• Well-known authors' growing clout allowed early agents to win them written contracts, more money, approval of changes, cover consultation, and reliable publication dates—perks that, with agitation by the Authors Guild, slowly trickled down to most other authors.

To be sure, publishers despised early agents and appealed to authors to shun the "parasites." *We're family, aren't we?* When appeals didn't work, publishers enlisted several New York periodicals to assert that they lost money on most books. In 1921, George Henry Doran (1869–1956), founder of a house eventually absorbed by Doubleday, told the *New York Herald*: "The author of a book is almost sure to make *some* money out of it; the publisher is about as sure not to."

When the PR blitz didn't work, publishers dug in their heels, following the example of Henry Holt, who as early as 1870 announced that he would never sign book contracts. *They impugn my integrity.* Holt insisted on handshake deals for forty years—until 1910.

Historian Tebbel observes agents were "inevitable, not only because of the economic factors involved but because the development of the mass market . . . gave authors a status, and in some cases an income, they had not enjoyed before. . . . There was a growing conviction that they [writers] did not have to endure the prevalent feeling among publishers that they should be grateful for what was given to them and not ask for more."

So many authors signed with agents that publishers had to deal with them. By World War I, agents had accomplished a great deal: written contracts, regular statements, and a share of subsidiary rights income. In addition, agents secured something new: advances, or prepublication payments to authors, previously as rare as Gutenberg Bibles. But advances were not gifts. They were *loans* against future royalties earned, repaid from book sales. If the advance is $1,000 and the book pays a royalty of one dollar per copy, the publisher must sell one thousand copies for the title to earn out before the author sees another dime.

Advances were an outgrowth of second book business economics. When publishers began hiring authors, they vied to sign those who penned big sellers. Agents monetized the competition by demanding money up front. As the decades passed, they were able to extend the practice to other authors, most of whom garnered small advances. Early on, if books didn't repay their advances, publishers wanted authors to reimburse them the difference, but agents insisted, *You want my superstar client? Take the risk.* Publishers weren't happy, but they wanted big names and caved. This tilted the book business one small notch back toward author-centrism. Today, the major publishers don't ask for money back if books don't repay advances (but read your contract).

However, despite agents' successes, like the Authors Guild, they were unable to coax publishers into transparent accounting and an industry-wide contract and royalty statement. The combined forces of agents, the Authors Guild, and activist big-name authors have been unable to win those demands to this day.

Agents advocate for authors, edit book proposals, vet contracts, and provide writing encouragement and shoulders to cry on. As they became fixtures in the book business, many authors thought, *Oh, good, my agent pays attention to the business side. I don't have to.*

The Emergence of Book Editing

During the first book business, editing, if any, was informal—friends' notes in manuscript margins. Printers had no interest in biblio-surgery. As noted, they had to be dragged into proofreading, and as hired guns, they quietly hoped authors would err on the side of verbosity. Longer books meant they could charge more for printing.

As the second book business developed and publishers began hiring authors, their first task was deciding whose books to publish. But publishers were—and still are—primarily entrepreneurs, not literary critics.

In addition, as the new model took hold, writers smelled opportunity: *Publishers pay us!* Publishers were deluged with manuscripts. Their small staffs felt overwhelmed.

A few took a leaf from newspapers and magazines and hired editors to wade into the stampede, hoping they would cull the cash cows. The most prominent early editor in chief, or "top" editor, was William Maxwell Evarts "Max" Perkins (1884–1947), hired by Scribner from the *New York Times* in 1910. Top editors focused on the big picture: in nonfiction, subject matter, organization, and incisiveness, and in fiction, characters, plot, pace, and style. Even today, Perkins is widely revered as one of the greatest American literary editors. His correspondence with authors, collected in *Editor to Author: The Letters of Maxwell E. Perkins* (1950), is notable for its kindness and thoughtfulness. Perkins's and other editors' big-picture suggestions became known as "developmental" editing.

Other publishers wondered if the new editors' efforts justified their salaries. Their value was hard to quantify, but houses that employed them quickly gained a better division of labor. Editors managed content, which freed publishers to focus on the increasingly complex business side. Companies that embraced the new org chart flourished, and by 1920, all the majors had top editors.

Publishers and top editors soon realized that book editing involved more than simply acquiring manuscripts and making developmental suggestions. Now that they paid for printing, publishers were eager to reduce their print bills—by cutting pages. Publishers have always let big names go on and on, but after World War I, they added something new to most authors' contracts: word limits.

Many authors run at the pen. As Mark Twain is widely reputed to have said, "I would have written a shorter story, but didn't have the time." (Actually, the quip originated with French mathematician Blaise Pascal (1623-1662) in reference to a lengthy letter.) Top editors had their hands full dealing with acquisitions and development, so "line" editing became an editorial specialty. Line editors streamline manuscripts, delete needless words and rearrange things to enhance clarity and flow. Line editors also put teeth into contractual length limits: *Cut your manuscript—or we will.*

By the 1920s, books had been proofread for more than a century, but proofreading was limited to typos and misspellings. In 1923, Louis Feipel of the Brooklyn Public Library examined seventy newly published titles and found them riddled with usage, punctuation, grammatical, and factual errors. He alerted the major publishers, arguing for a new editorial step between line editing and proofreading. Publishers ignored him.

Feipel turned to the news media. His report produced headlines. Authors, agents, booksellers, educators, and readers hailed him, while publishers squirmed, weighing embarrassment over all the errors against the cost of what the finicky librarian proposed. But it was the Roaring Twenties. The economy boomed, and publishers enjoyed the full flowering of the second book business. Surviving publishers prospered as never before and figured, *What the hell, we can invest a bit more in the product.* Feipel invented copyediting, which focuses on grammar, usage, and fact-checking. It quickly became standard.

Developmental, line, and copy editors were well worth their salaries, but like other industrialists, publishers squeezed their employees, turning publishing houses into intellectual sweatshops. During the Depression, unions decided that publishing was ripe for organizing. In 1934, editors at one major went on strike, and big names joined the picket line, among them Dashiell Hammett. The strikers' demands painted a dreary picture:

enough light to see manuscripts; no docking of pay for sick days; after a year, two weeks' paid vacation; and during sweltering New York summers, fans.

Dust Jackets and Blurbs: Covers Become Billboards

Until the 1880s, book covers were not particularly attractive, just unadorned leather or cloth-covered cardboard with title and author stamped in metal leaf. Then, in a few short years, technological innovations transformed book covers into mini-billboards that attracted book buyers' eyeballs and screamed *Buy me*!

Color had a lot to do with it. Color in books was as old as ancient Chinese scrolls and the illuminated manuscripts of the Middle Ages. But color printing on industrial presses appeared during the 1840s, when some printers added a second tone to highlight chapter titles or woodcuts. Three-color printing debuted in the 1880s; four-color (full-color), around World War I. In addition, in 1881, the halftone process revolutionized reproduction of art and photos by transforming pictures into patterns of easily printable graduated dots.

Color and halftones arrived not a moment too soon. With industrial printing, new releases soared and crowded bookseller shelves like never before. Naturally, publishers sought new ways to attract eyeballs. Around 1890, they jettisoned leather and began wrapping cardboard-cloth covers in paper dust jackets that featured bold, eye-catching full-color images.

Publishers loved dust jackets. The new covers cost less than leather, and imaginative cover artwork attracted buyers. Billboard dust jackets quickly became standard, much to the chagrin of leather merchants, who lost a lucrative market, and literary snobs, who insisted that color dust jackets looked garish, demeaned literature, and brought quality books one step closer to pulp fiction. Their critique added a new adage to the lexicon: "You can't tell a book by its cover."

Early dust jackets placed teaser copy on the back cover and left the flaps blank. Then publishers moved the copy to the flaps, freeing back covers for . . . what? *How about promotional quotes from notables?*

Celebrity book endorsements were nothing new. They dated from 1855, when Ralph Waldo Emerson congratulated Walt Whitman on *Leaves of Grass*: "I greet you at the beginning of a great career." Whitman's publisher touted the quote, and other publishers soon followed.

But breathless cover quotes raised howls from reviewers, librarians, educators, and bibliophiles. *Flagrant exaggerations! Insults to our intelligence!* As the kerfuffle over cover quotes raged, in 1907, Frank Gelett Burgess (1866–1951), a San Francisco satirist, released a collection of essays and, as a joke, included a ridiculously over-the-top dust-jacket quote from a fictional admirer, one Belinda Blurb. Ever since, promotional quotes have been called "blurbs."

I've blurbed friends' books generously, and they've graciously reciprocated. When one person does this, it's a kindness. But when every blurb calls every book God's gift, it becomes something else. Discerning readers take blurbs with a grain of salt, but without them covers look naked and authors look like amateurs. *What? She couldn't even get a few friends to say something nice?*

Book Reviews Gain (Some) Legitimacy

As industrial publishing produced cheaper books, and as books and top authors became more tightly woven into the cultural fabric, the mainstream media decided it was time to pay attention. The *New York Times* published its first book review in 1896, and other newspapers soon followed.

Meanwhile, would-be reviewers inundated publishers with requests for free copies, which vexed *Publishers Weekly*, whose editor opined in 1885: "There is, of course, a great deal of waste in the sending of books for review. . . . [P]ublishers, as a rule, are inclined to err in the direction of good-naturedly giving copies . . . instead of refusing requests whose denial may produce an irritation of future inconvenience"—that is, retaliatory pans of publishers' other titles. Nor was it clear that even glowing reviews actually sold books. Again, *PW* fretted: "The relation between criticism and sale is one which defies the most sagacious of publishers." It went on to cite a book that had been greeted "by a general chorus of praise, . . . yet total sales never reached the number of press copies sent out."

After World War I, book reviews spread throughout the nation's periodicals and gained credibility, thanks in part to Virginia Kirkus (1893–1980), an English teacher who became an editor at Harper and, in 1933, launched Virginia Kirkus Bookshop Service, which published brief reviews of soon-to-be-published titles for booksellers. In 1969 it became *Kirkus Reviews* and gained a reputation for trustworthiness.

But pundits continued to wonder about ulterior motives among reviewers and the editors who selected them, while publishers continued to wonder if reviews—even raves—actually sold books.

= 13 =

The Fraught Debut of Bestseller Lists and a "Line of Type"

Publishers called popular titles "big books," not "bestsellers." The phrasing changed in 1899, when Harry Thurston Peck (1856–1914), editor of the New York literary magazine the *Bookman*, introduced the first bestseller list.

It's not clear how Peck conceived the idea, nor why he limited his list to fiction, but one thing is certain: authors, educators, booksellers, and reviewers unanimously condemned him, insisting that books' sales were irrelevant. The only valid metric was "literary merit," as judged by "quality" readers who had "taste"—in other words, the opinions of the intellectual elite.

ONLY ONE BOOK IN 13,500 BECOMES A BESTSELLER

To be considered real, books must bear International Standard Book Numbers (ISBNs). In 2021, publishing houses accounted for 400,000 ISBNs, and self-publishers, 2.3 million—a total of 2.7 million ISBNs that year. The New York Times bestseller list includes around two hundred titles a year. So, bestsellers account for approximately one release in 13,500. Imagine Madison Square Garden or a similar arena. If authors filled every seat, one would have a book on the bestseller list. How many copies must a title sell to rank number one on the New York Times bestseller list? That's not clear. But to hit number one on Amazon, a book must sell at least five thousand copies in twenty-four hours.

Controversy over the *Bookman*'s bestseller list raged for a decade, but Peck, an upper-crust Columbia University graduate and classics scholar, stuck to his populist guns. It didn't take long for publishers to notice that books anointed bestsellers enjoyed reliable sales boosts. Apparently, readers valued what others read.

In 1911, *PW* launched two bestseller lists, fiction and nonfiction. The *New York Times* published its first list in 1931, but only for titles sold in New York City. In 1942, its list went national and quickly became the touchstone. Ever since, the phrase "*New York Times* bestseller" has brought considerable attention—media coverage, author interviews, and more visible bookstore placement—and a reliable spike in sales.

Mysteries of the Bestseller List

During one week in 2008, when Stieg Larsson's *The Girl with the Dragon Tattoo* was a bestseller, various lists ranked it number one, two, five, and seven. Which raises a question: How are bestseller lists compiled?

Nobody's talking. Decisions about the *New York Times* list are as secret as the formula for Coca-Cola. Not even *Times* book-review editors know. The paper's news surveys department compiles the list. Formulas for other prominent lists—*PW*, the *Los Angeles Times*, and the *Washington Post*—are equally hush-hush, ostensibly to discourage gaming their systems.

But secrecy invites as much corruption as it prevents.

The one fact publicly known is that bestseller lists begin with sales reports from selected bookstores. But booksellers aren't disinterested observers: they know that a spot on the list spurs sales.

Say a bookseller orders cases of a supposedly hot new title whose sales fizzle, meaning a big shipping bill for returns. However, if that bookseller is a "reporting store," there's another alternative: call it a hit. If it makes the list, that means more sales and fewer returns.

Open or secret, any system can be subverted. It's clear that bestseller lists can be manipulated. Nowadays, some books ascend to various lists out of nowhere. How? Authors or publishers appeal to fans or contract with marketing firms to buy enough copies to get there. One outfit, ResultSource of San Diego, has used this strategy to create several bestsellers. The company reportedly charges up to $200,000 per title, plus the cost of several thousand books. That's way beyond the means of most authors, but for the few with that money, the expense might be worth it. If the *Times* lists a book for even one day, in perpetuity it's a "*New York Times* bestseller." That sells books.

Today, bestseller lists are a fact of life. But if *Uncle Tom's Cabin* heralded the two tracks of publishing—big books and everything else—bestseller lists sharpened the distinction, elevating the few to pedestals while leaving the vast majority in the dust.

THE POPULARITY EFFECT: ARE BESTSELLERS GREAT? OR JUST LUCKY?
The controversy surrounding bestseller lists highlights an enduring debate in the arts. Do the best books (or songs, plays, movies, etc.) become the most popular? And if not, why not?

Three Columbia University sociologists, Duncan J. Watts, Peter Dodds, and Matthew Salganik, investigated this question using an ingenious experiment. They divided fourteen thousand participants into eight groups and offered them free downloads of forty-eight songs by unknown rock bands—if they agreed to rate them. One group, the uninfluenced, rated the songs entirely by themselves. The other seven, the influenced, judged the songs but knew how one or more of the other groups rated them.

Ratings by the uninfluenced were consistently middling. They liked some songs better than others but issued few pans or raves. They called most "eh" to "okay."

The influenced, however, either loved the songs or hated them. Middling ratings largely disappeared. Listeners privy to others' opinions rated already favored songs much higher and disparaged tunes much lower. In each influenced group, if a few initial listeners liked a song, it was much more likely to become very popular, but if a handful of early listeners were unenthusiastic, it was doomed.

The uninfluenced rated one song number twenty-six of forty-eight. But in one influenced group, early praise propelled it to number one, while in another, initial disdain sank it to forty. In other words, among the influenced, ratings depended heavily on a few initial opinions.

Of course, we're all heavily influenced. We constantly hear what others think, and their views color ours. As a result, popularity often has less to do with quality than luck. Works lucky enough to garner early praise, including books, generally become more popular. That's why publishers crave prepublication buzz. But good books denied early praise have scant chance in a marketplace largely defined by rocketing out of the gate.

Offset Printing and a Line of Type

In 1875, hoping to reproduce artwork more cost-effectively, an English printer stopped printing directly from metal plates and transferred ink from the plate to a rubber cylinder, printing from that. The new process, offset printing, aka photo-offset, photolithography, or litho, enhanced image quality.

In 1903, the American printer Ira Rubel adapted the process to text. Offset presses, larger and more complex than ever, could print books beautifully in the blink of an eye. As offset became the industry standard, the few publishing houses that still owned presses sold them and contracted with offset printers, ending once and for all the 250-year marriage of printing and publishing.

Paper also evolved, becoming lighter and cheaper to ship. Lightweight paper, or onionskin, had existed for a century, but it didn't work for books. Printing on one side "bled" to the other. In 1902, a new paper appeared that was opaque, lightweight, and cheap. In 1850, paper accounted for 20 percent of books' manufacturing cost, but the marvelous new paper slashed it to just 7 percent. The new paper quickly became standard.

Typesetting also became easier, faster, and cheaper. From Gutenberg until the late nineteenth century, compositors set type by hand one character at a time. Capital letters were stored in a box, or case, at head height. Other letters filled a case at chest height—hence "upper-" and "lowercase" letters.

In 1884, a machine appeared that set a whole line at once. These "line of type" devices soon became known as "line-o'-type" and then "linotype." Subsequent innovations allowed almost instant typesetting of entire pages.

Bindings improved as well. Sewing became almost obsolete thanks to better glues and mechanized "perfect" bindings that produced books with flat spines ideal for printing titles. By World War I, handcrafted books had almost disappeared.

Savage v. Neely:
Authors Gain the Right to Audit Publishers

Bestseller lists demonstrated that some books sold remarkably well. Agents and the Authors Guild harnessed this new information to agitate for greater financial transparency. But publishers refused to open their ledgers. *Publishers Weekly* endorsed the publishers' position: "No reputable publisher would be so dishonest or so foolish as to lie and perjure himself, directly or by proxy, in this matter of accounting to authors for royalties." Nineteenth-century courts endorsed publishers' financial secrecy on the grounds that business records were proprietary. The fox guarded the henhouse.

As soon as publishers offered authors contracts, some worked to wring every advantage from them. In 1905, Walter Page, a founder of Doubleday, released *A Publisher's Confession*, which advocated hand-cuff contracts that lasted the author's lifetime, like baseball before free agency.

In 1910, at a Boston meeting of the International Publishers Association, an English publisher called agents bloodsuckers who were draining the life from the book business. Across Massachusetts, the *Springfield Republican* replied editorially: "It was [for the sake] of defending the producer, that is to say the author, from the predatory middleman, that is to say the publisher, that the author's agent came into vogue." All this to limit "the greed of publishers."

Which brings us to *Savage v. Neely*. Colonel Richard Henry Savage (1846–1903) was a West Point graduate who wrote wildly popular, but critically excoriated, action-adventure pulp paperbacks loosely based on his military career. In 1896, Savage sued his publisher, Frank Neely, for royalty fraud, demanding all plates and $12,000 in damages ($400,000 today). Savage claimed that Neely had boasted of selling more than one hundred thousand copies of his books, while his royalty statements showed sales of only twenty copies a month. Savage demanded Neely's records, but the publisher refused. Savage sued, and the New York appellate court ruled in his favor, holding that authors had the right to audit publishers. Neely quickly settled out of court.

However, few authors could afford audits. Occasionally, the big names sued, and like *Savage*, their cases settled out of court contingent on the authors' perpetual silence. I spoke with an accountant who had conducted seventy-five royalty audits for authors. In every case, he said, he found errors in the publishers' favor to the tune of 15 to 20 percent of the amounts his clients received. The problem: depending on books' sales, royalty audits cost $10,000 to $20,000 per title. They're feasible for only big names.

If your royalties are north of, say, $40,000 in a year and you opt to audit, I have one heartfelt request. Please refuse any gag order. Go public with your results through the Authors Guild. If your publisher paid you honestly, the world should know the house is scrupulous. If not, the publisher should be publicly branded a thief.

The (Re)Birth of Sales Forces

After World War I, the economy slipped into recession and book sales fell. Publishers who had giddily sold mountains of titles to Carnegie libraries suddenly had second thoughts. Library patrons were *borrowing* books instead of *buying* them, and a single copy could be borrowed forever. Even more distressing, purveyors of pulp began releasing classics on coarse paper for as little as a nickel, taking a bite out of publishers' backlist sales. One line of pulp classics, Little Blue Books, sold three hundred million copies between the World Wars.

The majors struck back using the latest technologies. In 1927, shortly after Charles Lindbergh's solo transatlantic flight made him a sensation, the newspaper syndicate United Press assembled an instant biography of Lucky Lindy and delivered it on a Monday to D. Appleton & Company.

By that Friday, the house had produced a 250-page book with twenty-four photographs and a color dust jacket. (D. Appleton became Appleton-Century-Crofts, now owned by the English media conglomerate Pearson.)

Meanwhile, publishers continued to struggle with moving books from warehouses to bookstores. In 1913, the *Atlantic Monthly* called distribution publishing's "chief problem." *Publishers Weekly* concurred: "The world is still looking for a publisher who will 'discover and invent' a new method which shall be practical and effective for the distribution of books."

And yet, the book business thrived. In 1925, American publishers released a record 8,173 titles, and for the first time, average print run topped two thousand.

By this time, most businesses had telephones. As phones proliferated, publishers supplemented catalogues with calls to cajole booksellers to take more copies of more titles. But phone calls accomplished only so much, and as books proliferated, publishers toyed with reviving an idea that had failed before the Civil War, namely book travelers: roving salesmen who importuned booksellers to stock new releases.

Back in 1850, Harper had sent Charles B. Norton (1825–1891) on a four-thousand-mile ship, rail, and stagecoach trip to booksellers in two dozen cities from Rochester to New Orleans. But he sold few books and that was the end of it. (Subsequently, Norton launched *Norton's Literary Gazette and Publishers' Circular*, which became *Publishers Weekly*.)

After 1900, a few publishers resurrected book travelers. Others called them crazy. Their salaries, commissions, and expenses really added up. But this time, improved transportation and an increasingly competitive book business turned the idea into a winner. Sales reps moved so many books that sales forces quickly became standard.

= 14 =

"Goodbye Forever, Mrs. Weathersby, I've Joined Book of the Month"

In 1902, with 92 percent of Americans literate and publishers releasing a record 1,797 novels, Jules Verne (1828–1905) lamented, "I do not think there will be any novels . . . in fifty or a hundred years from now. . . . They are not necessary, and even now their merit and their interest are fast declining."

A decade later, in 1913, with literacy at 94 percent, publishers released a record 12,230 new titles, but *Leslie's Weekly* moaned, "People don't read books any more. . . . Who has time to read books nowadays? . . . Molders of public opinion may write books, but read them? Never! . . . Books were made for other days when men thought and statesmen studied."

During the 1920s, predictions of books' imminent demise soared with the arrival of two wildly popular new media: radio and movies. Guglielmo Marconi (1874–1937) successfully transmitted the first radio signals in 1895. The following year, the nation's first motion-picture screening took place in New York City. By the 1920s, radio and movies were cultural staples, and anxious bibliophiles doubted that books could survive them.

In 1925, the *Atlantic Monthly* opined, "Human beings have only a certain maximum of leisure, and, if they spend an evening . . . listening to the radio, there is no time left for a good book." In 1927, *Library Journal* stated, "Pessimistic defenders of the book . . . are wont to contrast the actual process of reading with the lazy and passive contemplation of the screen or listening to wireless, and to prophecy [sic] the death of the book." And the Columbia University professor Walter Pitkin (1878–1953), a prominent cultural critic, said, "It is hard to see how they can hold their own for another generation. The primary motive for reading books and magazines is entertainment. [As radio and movies] are increasing and becoming more and more refined, magazines and books are losing out."

Au contraire. Books and publishing not only survived, they thrived. Reading brought unique pleasure that could not be duplicated by other media—deeper and longer lasting. No wonder the book is almost always better than the movie.

Movie Rights and Book Clubs

Despite the twin threats of radio and movies, the 1920s were sweet for the book business. In 1921, the publisher George Doran told the *New York Herald*: "Never in the history of literature in America has there been such increase in the number of readers, or, as this may or may not indicate, so widespread an interest in all kinds of books." The following year, *PW* editorialized: "No one can circulate among publishers, without feeling that there is an unbounded optimism among them, founded on the sales of the first six months and the orders that have been coming in."

And a new goose laid golden eggs. Hollywood producers began paying to turn books into movies. Before film, "subsidiary rights" meant foreign sales, usually for pennies. Movies turned "sub" rights into a bonanza. In 1920, the rights to *Huckleberry Finn* sold for $1,000 ($12,000 today). *PW* launched regular coverage of book-to-film deals in 1923, and by the end of the decade, bestsellers' movie rights often brought six figures—meaning publishers might earn more from film rights than from sales of the book. Even more surprising, movies *spurred* book sales. When the movie appeared, sales of the book often soared. And if hit movies were produced from original screenplays, their scripts could be turned into books that often sold well. The first "novelization" was *King Kong* (1932).

Movies helped publishing in another way: bigger posters. Spurred by movie studios, in 1927, printers developed a cheap way to produce large color posters. Publishers adopted the practice, filling bookstores with movie-style posters touting bestsellers.

During the 1920s, another new sub-rights opportunity emerged: book clubs. Mail-order bookselling had been around since Ben Franklin, but the Book-of-the-Month Club (founded in 1926) and the Literary Guild (1927) changed it. With publishers releasing more titles than ever, book clubs did the opposite. They offered only a few dozen bestsellers and a smattering of other titles.

Book clubs rarely sold publishers' editions. They licensed rights, then printed their own editions on paper one rung up from pulp. They prospered by selling at well below retail, starting with a hard-to-resist teaser: four books for one dollar if members bought several more at the clubs' low prices. The formula proved so successful that in short order, specialty book clubs popped up for romance, mystery, science fiction, history, gardening, politics, and children's books.

But book clubs infuriated bibliophiles. The *Bookman* castigated members as "too feeble-minded, too lazy, or too busy to make their own choice of a book." The *New Yorker* crystallized the moment with a cartoon showing a matron telling a frowning librarian, "Goodbye forever, Mrs. Weathersby. I've joined Book of the Month." Book clubs also sucked sales from independent booksellers, pushing some into bankruptcy.

How Radio, Movies, and Television Affected Reading

Throughout the 1800s, novels aimed at women dominated book publishing, primarily romance fiction, the perennial leader, and a niche publishers dubbed "H&J," home and Jesus—convoluted multigenerational sagas of reckless youths who eventually settled into God-fearing domesticity while raising wild children and grandchildren who followed in their footsteps.

While the new media did not destroy the book business, radio, movies, and later TV ended fiction's dominance. The conventional wisdom declared that electronic media met much of the public's need for storytelling, so readers felt less compelled to buy novels. Not that fiction died—far from it. During the twentieth century, many readers read nothing but novels, many of which bibliophiles return to again and again: *The Great Gatsby, Brave New World, Gone with the Wind, The Grapes of Wrath, 1984, The Catcher in the Rye, Invisible Man, The Old Man and the Sea, Lord of the Flies,* the Lord of the Rings trilogy, *To Kill a Mockingbird, Catch-22, The Shining, The Color Purple, The Handmaid's Tale, Beloved,* the Harry Potter series.

And yet by the 1990s, fiction accounted for only 15 percent of trade book sales.

Simon Meets Schuster and Publishers Wonder if Advertising Sells Books

In 1928, publishing celebrated its biggest year yet: 9,176 new releases. Publishers still failed regularly, but a love of books, cultural cachet, and the possibility of hitting it bigger than ever spurred many neophytes to try publishing:

• After graduating from Harvard, Harold Guinzburg (1899–1961) befriended George Oppenheimer (1900–1977), who worked for Knopf. In 1925, they launched Viking Press.

• Bennett Cerf (1898–1971) came from a wealthy New York family, graduated from Columbia University in 1920, and quickly worked his way up to vice president of a then prominent publisher, Boni & Liveright. B&L released the lucrative Modern Library of the World's Best Books series of cheap hardback editions of a large catalogue of classics. But Horace Liveright's alcoholism destroyed the house. In 1925, it went belly-up. As it failed, VP Cerf and his partner, Donald Klopfer (1902–1986), bought the rights to Modern Library for next to nothing. Then Cerf made a splash announcing that the phoenix rising from B&L's ashes would publish books without any strategy, "at random," hence Random House. Cerf cultivated a persona as a brilliant, carefree bon vivant, but he was a shrewd businessman. He could prattle about publishing books at random because, from its inception, Random House made steady money from its Modern Library backlist.

•Richard Simon (1899–1960) and Max Schuster (1897–1970) were an odd couple. Simon grew up in Manhattan a well-to-do music lover. After graduating from Columbia University, he sold books for a major publisher, then quit to sell pianos. Schuster was the son of poor immigrants who also graduated from Columbia. After knocking around newspapers, he became the editor of a trade magazine with offices in the building that housed Simon's piano showroom. Schuster declined Simon's entreaties to buy a Steinway, but they became friends and talked publishing. In 1924, they rented an office. The morning after their new venture's name was painted on the door, they found it vandalized. Beneath "Simon and Schuster, Publishers," someone had scrawled, "Of what?" They had no idea.

But during Schuster's newspaper years, he'd taken a fancy to crossword puzzles, first published in 1913. S&S released the first book-length crossword collection, packaging it with an eraser-tipped pencil. In short order, that book and several sequels sold more than a million copies, making the two twentysomething publishers rich and financing their move into trade publishing. (Richard Simon's daughter is the singer-songwriter Carly Simon.)

Like their printer predecessors, the young bucks of industrial publishing were businessmen who wanted to strike it rich. But they also loved books and enjoyed the stature that publishing granted. Many became prominent. One became a TV celebrity. From 1951 to 1967, Bennett Cerf appeared as a panelist on the game show *What's My Line?*

Does Advertising Sell Books?

In 1859, when *A Tale of Two Cities* appeared, it was scarcely advertised and the first bestseller list was decades in the future. But its newspaper serialization created major buzz—*You must read this!*—which spurred sales of the full-length version. Clearly, word-of-mouth recommendations sold books.

When bestseller lists appeared, they were one step removed from word of mouth, but they too reliably sold books. However, good reviews, also one step from personal endorsements, had maddeningly unpredictable effects. Well-reviewed books often bombed, and critically scorned titles often soared. Book people scratched their heads, wondering if something other than word of mouth and bestseller status might spur sales, just as advertising became an industry.

Book advertising got off to a slow start. Colonial printers touted their services in periodicals they published and sometimes mentioned books they'd printed. After the Civil War, publishers advertised book fairs, lines of cheap paperbacks, and opportunities to work as subscription agents, but not individual titles, a position endorsed by most authors and bibliophiles, who viewed book advertising as vulgar.

During the early nineteenth century, newspaper and magazine advertising consisted of classifieds and business-card-size notices—nothing large, flashy, or eye-catching. Then in 1836, a French newspaper offered big, visually arresting "display" ads. They cost more, but readers loved them and couldn't buy enough of display ads' products, which convinced more advertisers to buy more of the new advertisements. Display ads boosted the newspaper publisher's income, allowing him to cut his newsstand price, outsell competing newspapers, and gain readers. More readers meant more eyeballs seeing the glitzy ads, a "higher rate base," which enabled the publisher to charge more for them. The French publisher coined money, and periodicals around the world quickly adopted his model. By World War I, advertising was a big business. Many ad agencies clustered in New York City, and as advertising people rubbed shoulders with book people, publishers' attitudes shifted.

Initially, publishers thought *booksellers* should advertise new titles. Of course, the latter saw things differently. In 1885, the *New York Times* agreed: "Authors frequently complain that their books do not sell. . . . The reason is plain. Publishers have no real conception of the art of advertising." But advertising cost a fortune.

The early twentieth century saw the introduction of many new consumer products whose manufacturers advertised heavily: vacuum cleaners (1901), electric washing machines (c. 1904), Corn Flakes (1906), the Model T (1908), toasters (1909), and refrigerators (1913). Meanwhile, the cultural identity of hardcover books was changing. They had evolved from luxury items for the rich into icons of upper-middle-class prosperity, and by World War I, books were on their way to becoming just another box of breakfast cereal. Authors, agents, and booksellers exhorted publishers to advertise books as if they were All-Bran (1916).

Starting in the 1890s, a few publishers tried placards on New York City buses and subways and display ads in *PW* and the *New York Times*. The Sunday *Times Book Review* debuted in 1896. Throughout the twentieth century, it accounted for 20 percent of trade book advertising. Publishers also experimented with billboards and discount coupons. But many publishers considered advertising a waste of money, and they advertised much less than other businesses of comparable size—which authors and booksellers derided as penny-wise and pound-foolish.

After World War I, publishers tried a different approach, trumpeting not individual titles but reading. In a rare collaboration, in 1920, sixteen houses and dozens of booksellers chipped in to buy newspaper ads: *Curl up with good books*—an early example of "co-op" advertising, in which publishers and booksellers shared costs for mutual benefit. They raised $100,000 and bought ads from coast to coast. But the results were disappointing (or at least difficult to measure), and the campaign fizzled.

By the mid-1920s, publishers concluded that advertising didn't *launch* book sales, but if titles were already selling, advertising helped. They used the analogy of a cart mired in mud. When the cart is stuck, a dozen shoulders to the wheel can't budge it. But if the cart starts moving, a little push keeps it rolling.

What was selling? Bestsellers. Publishers advertised them and the ads worked. Publishers also stumbled on a corollary insight. Sales could usually be boosted if ads promised *future* success—hence proclamations of "Third Big Printing before Publication!" and "Soon to Be a Major Motion Picture!"

And if assertions of brisk sales begat more sales, why not exaggerate *all* sales figures? Publishers did—until 2001, when Nielsen, the TV-audience auditor, introduced its BookScan auditing service, ending decades of what a less delicate author might call lies. Of course, all authors wanted *their* books advertised and couldn't understand why publishers pushed only bestsellers. It's no different today. Want a sure sign of author naiveté? Anyone who complains *The publisher didn't advertise my book.*

Small Presses Develop a Viable Niche

As industrial publishing allowed large houses to dominate the bestseller list and establish recognizable brand names—Random House, Simon & Schuster, etc.—a few entrepreneurs combined elements of industrial publishing and the almost abandoned model of handcrafted books, becoming the predecessors of today's independent presses. By the 1920s, these iconoclasts were producing exquisite, large-format art books, the forerunners of today's coffee table books. Some eventually branched into poetry and fiction.

American expatriates in Paris founded two of the most celebrated early small presses. Sylvia Beach (1887–1962) owned a bookshop, Shakespeare and Company, on the Left Bank and, in 1919, added a publishing arm that released James Joyce's *Ulysses*. In 1927, Harry Crosby (1898–1929) and his wife, Caresse (1891–1970), founded Black Sun Press, which published Ernest Hemingway, Ezra Pound, Oscar Wilde, D. H. Lawrence, and T. S. Eliot.

= 16 =

Under Pressure: The Great Depression Changes Bookselling

After the 1929 stock market crash, the Depression hammered publishing like nothing before or since. Books weren't necessities, and when the economy tanked, consumers stopped buying. Libraries also cut way back, their budgets slashed. Department store book sections, which accounted for almost half of trade sales, contracted or disappeared. Sales plummeted. Dozens of publishers and hundreds of booksellers failed.

At the first hint of tumbling sales, publishers cut prices from $2.50 to $1 (today, from $33 to $13), triggering a price war that lasted throughout the 1930s. Price cutting pulled sales out of free fall but also opened publishers to attack. The nation's newspapers seized on the discounts as proof that greedy publishers had been gouging consumers all along. Publishers hardly advertised, so newspapers risked little loss of income lambasting them. As sales plunged, publishers reduced acquisitions and print runs. From 1929 to 1933, releases dropped 21 percent, and print runs by half.

Increasingly desperate, publishers and booksellers revived their earlier effort to promote reading. Booksellers filled their windows with publisher-financed movie-style posters heralding "Books for a Thinking

America." Publishers also pulled other old rabbits out of the hat: book fairs and discount coupons in newspapers. But buyers' wallets remained firmly shut. Publishers became frantic.

In 1931, a consortium of majors hired the public relations pioneer Edward Bernays (1891–1995) to boost book buying. His suggestion: demonize book borrowing. The consortium sponsored a contest to coin a pejorative term for it. Entries included "bookbum," "booklooter," and "bookaneer." A panel of critics selected the winner, "book sneak." But the term didn't catch on. Book borrowing was as old as printing and was the backbone of libraries. The public saw nothing wrong with it. More publishers and independents failed, and more department stores stopped selling books.

Meanwhile, like sharks circling a foundering ship, pulp publishers sensed opportunity. In addition to genre releases, they reprinted public-domain classics and even recent bestsellers. Publishers and booksellers howled about "trash editions," but the success of pulp paperbacks during the Depression planted a seed that eventually germinated into the mass-market paperback.

Other entrepreneurs also saw possibilities. If people wouldn't *buy* books, perhaps they'd *rent* them at, say, ten cents a month. In 1933, Lawrence Hoyt (1902–1982) left Simon & Schuster and opened a rental library in Bridgeport, Connecticut, called Walden Book Company. It was touch and go. Even a dime a month stretched many Depression budgets. But Walden survived, and as the economy improved, Hoyt opened more rental locations, some in storefronts, others in space leased from department stores that had killed their book sections.

Booksellers cut purchases to the bone. Publishers found themselves with warehouses full of books no one wanted, while printers demanded payment and threatened lawsuits. More publishers failed, and the survivors realized that unless something changed quickly, they were history.

Ironically, the bloodbath of the Depression united two old and bitter foes: independent booksellers and department stores. The indies hated department stores, but the two camps also shared some resentments. Publishers had always insisted on payment up front, refusing returns and credit for unsold copies.

Publishers pleaded with booksellers: *Please take more books.*

Booksellers: *Sorry, we can't.*

Publishers: *What can we do to place more books on your shelves?*

The department stores and independents spoke with one loud voice: *You really want to know? Ship books on consignment and accept returns for full credit.*

Publishers: *Consignment? Full credit? Unthinkable!*

But faced with horrendous losses and imminent ruin, the majors caved. In 1930, Putnam, Norton, and Knopf bit the bullet, and by 1933, all the majors had agreed to the new terms, not exactly consignment but something close. True consignment involves sellers paying only when merchandise sells, now called "pay on scan." Booksellers paid nothing to acquire books, but the new system required "net thirty," meaning booksellers were obliged to pay publishers in thirty days, though in practice, many took longer. If books didn't sell, booksellers were free to return them for full credit, though booksellers had to pay to ship returns.

For publishers, selling on consignment was bad, but full credit for returns was worse. For eighty years, they'd been drowning in remainders. Now they had to contend with more. Shortly after acquiescing, Alfred Knopf watched books being packaged for shipment and famously sniffed, "Gone today, here tomorrow." To compensate for additional returns, publishers raised prices as soon as they could. As the economy picked up, new releases and print runs rebounded, then soared during World War II, despite paper restrictions. Publishing was publisher-centric, but the Depression shifted the balance of power a bit toward booksellers.

SHOULD LIBRARIES PAY AUTHORS ROYALTIES?

During the Depression, publishers complained that library borrowing hurt sales. Authors have a similar beef with libraries. When radio stations broadcast recorded music, they pay royalties to artists. But when readers borrow library books, authors get nothing.

Librarians counter that radio stations obtain music for free, so it's fair that they pay at the back end. But libraries pay for books up front and shouldn't have to pony up royalties later. Librarians also contended that paying royalties would reduce acquisitions, hurting authors more.

Perhaps, but in thirty-three countries, libraries pay royalties, a practice known as the "public lending right" (PLR). Denmark originated the PLR in 1946. Most other countries adopted it by 1960. Participants include the UK, Canada, Germany, Sweden, Norway, Finland, Denmark, Belgium, Austria, Israel, Australia, and New Zealand. Some instituted the PLR to compensate authors for sales lost to library borrowing. Others view it as government support for the arts. Whatever the reason, in participating countries, when library patrons borrow books, authors make money.

Libraries pay either per borrower or per book. Payments are modest. Canada pays per book, $50 to $4,500 per title per year, depending on how many copies Canadian libraries hold and how often they're borrowed.

Since 1979, the Authors Guild has lobbied Congress to institute a public lending right, so far, to no avail.

This son of a librarian loves libraries, but I wish the United States would adopt the PLR.

Cheap Paperbacks Go Mainstream

After World War I, as innovations cut book prices, the growing middle class accumulated home libraries. However, the new book buyers faced a dilemma: hardcovers were still expensive, but pulp paperbacks were manufactured so poorly that they quickly fell apart. Then Robert de Graff (1895–1981) had an idea.

A top salesman at Doubleday, de Graff believed the company's books, priced at $2.98, were too expensive for Depression-traumatized buyers. In 1936, he quit to become president of a reprint house that sold books for $1.98, but he yearned to produce good books cheaper. In 1938, de Graff resigned and visited England, where Penguin published small, well-manufactured, pocket-size paperbacks for pennies. De Graff believed that approach would work in the United States.

Looking for partners, he visited his publishing pals. They called him crazy, insisting it was impossible to produce well-manufactured paperbacks cheap. Besides, only working-class readers bought pocket-size books, and they shopped at drugstores, not bookstores.

De Graff persisted and, in 1939, partnered with Simon & Schuster. The company they launched, Pocket Books, introduced Americans to mass-market paperbacks—well printed on decent paper with color covers and perfect bound with strong glue—for just a quarter. Pocket's first titles included works by Shakespeare, *Wuthering Heights*, and *Bambi*. In short order, the company was selling millions of copies a year.

Mass-market paperbacks suffered from paper restrictions during World War II, but as soon as rationing ceased, sales rebounded—and Pocket Books faced competition. In 1945, Ian Ballantine (1916–1995), his wife, Betty (1919–2019), and two partners launched Bantam Books. In 1952, the Ballantines left and formed Ballantine Books. Other mass-market publishers soon followed: Fawcett, Signet, and Warner.

Like pulp paperbacks, mass-market titles were distributed not by book wholesalers but by magazine distributors. And like magazines, if they didn't fly off wire racks at newsstands, pharmacies, grocery stores, and, later, supermarkets, they were quickly replaced. Meanwhile, bookstores refused to stock mass-market titles. Booksellers clung to their hoary tradition of offering only hardcover books.

> **A GUARANTEED BOON FOR READING: WAR**
> During the Civil War, families and civic organizations on both sides of the conflict shipped hundreds of thousands of pulp paperbacks to their fighting sons, many of whom learned to read in the military. By World War II, troops received millions of early mass-market paperbacks for free, a program that turned many young soldiers into lifelong readers and helped popularize the then-new format. Books in all formats were sent to troops during the Korean and Vietnam Wars. More recently, during the Iraq and Afghanistan Wars, despite computer games, the internet, streaming video, and Skype, many soldiers curled up with books.

Paperback Profiteering

Initially, Pocket Books published only public-domain classics. But after World War II, mass-market publishers began reprinting books by living authors, who, along with their hardcover publishers, demanded royalties. But how much? Hardbacks paid 10 percent or more. So, what did mass-market publishers offer? On the first 150,000 copies, 4 percent, and beyond that, 6 percent, split between authors and the original publishers—so 2 to 3 percent each. Authors hit the roof.

At a 1953 Authors Guild forum, Ian Ballantine rhapsodized that, for no extra effort, mass-market reprints gave authors "the thrill of increased readership." The authors in attendance were all for more readers, but they called his royalty offer insulting.

A Guild study group concluded: "Our investigation leaves no doubt that reprint publishers have been getting an enormous slice of the money, a larger share of which should be going to those who create the product. Authors are being seriously underpaid for reprint rights."

In this fight, authors had an unexpected ally, their hardcover publishers, who split mass-market royalties and also considered the proposed rate ludicrous. Book contracts gave them control of subsidiary rights, and hardcover publishers told the mass-market houses that they wouldn't authorize reprints unless Bantam et al. upped the ante. The reprinters relented. Today, mass-market houses (all now absorbed into major publishers) typically pay 7 percent. While that was an improvement over the initial offer, it was still less than 10 percent, which left authors and agents grumbling.

Seduction of the Innocent

By the 1930s, it was clear that books and reading had more than held up against the phonograph, radio, and movies. After the Depression, as book sales rebounded, bibliophiles confronted two new dastardly nemeses: Superman and Batman.

Newspapers had published comic strips since the 1890s, but in 1939, the first freestanding comic book, *Superman*, debuted, followed a year later by *Batman*. They and other superheroes proved so popular with kids, especially boys, that anxious educators feared for book reading and banned comics from schools. Many parents confiscated them.

Anti-comics hysteria culminated in 1954 with the psychiatrist Fredric Wertham's book *Seduction of the Innocent*, which argued that comic books corrupted young minds. Ironically, one author who grew up perverted by comic books set a literary novel in that realm, and in 2001, Michael Chabon won the Pulitzer Prize for *The Amazing Adventures of Kavalier & Clay*.

= 17 =

The Kid Who Singlehandedly Changed the Book Business

The Quiet Dawn of Corporate Publishing

After the Depression, surviving trade publishers bounced back and prospered. They employed an average of twenty-one people and, in 1940, released 11,328 new titles. Department stores sold half of trade books, with independents at 25 percent and the rest sold at drug and stationery stores and specialty outlets (e.g., knitting books at yarn shops). In 1943, *Time* magazine reported that in the thirty years since 1914, American book purchases had soared from 175 million copies to a staggering 300 million, helped considerably by all the books sent to soldiers during World War II. *Time* called 1943 "the most remarkable [year] in the 150-year-old history of U.S. publishing," noting that book buying had spread from the wealthy to "the whole vast literate population."

But World War II squeezed publishers in a new vise: paper rationing. They stretched their allotments by using smaller type, thinner margins, and less space between lines ("leading," pronounced *ledding*). Publishers also bought paper on the black market. Paper restrictions were lifted in 1945—just in time for two million veterans to enter college on the G.I. Bill and send textbook sales through the roof.

By the end of World War II, the nation's 648 book publishers, including several dozen New York majors, were grossing $425 million a year. By the standards of the great industrialists, book publishing remained small, idiosyncratic, and entrepreneurial. But annual revenue approaching a half billion dollars piqued the interest of a few corporate chieftains, especially those with ties to the biggest booksellers, department stores. In 1944, Marshall Field III (1893–1956), grandson of the Chicago department store magnate and owner of several newspapers and radio stations, bought Simon & Schuster and Pocket Books.

The corporate invasion of publishing unnerved bibliophiles, who feared that Field might censor the companies' lists. It also scared publishers. Field had deep pockets. Would he slash prices and sell books at a loss until he'd driven them all out of business, then, in classic monopoly fashion, raise prices and clean up?

All Field did was provide operating capital and expand the two companies' joint distribution network. After his death, his estate executors sold them in 1957. But corporate publishing was just beginning.

Enter Epstein

In 1953, Jason Epstein was a recent Columbia University graduate working in publishing—temporarily, he thought—as an editorial assistant at Doubleday. He lived in Greenwich Village, a short walk from the funky but glorious (and now defunct) Eighth Street Bookshop, which counted among its patrons Jack Kerouac, Susan Sontag, E. E. Cummings, Edward Albee, Allen Ginsberg, and Amiri Baraka. To Epstein's wide young eyes, the place was paradise. He visited after work, sometimes lingering for hours. But his editorial assistant's salary paid so little (forty-five dollars a week) that he couldn't afford hardcovers, and that was all Eighth Street Bookshop stocked.

One day Epstein asked the store's owners if they might be interested in selling less expensive paperback editions of their hardcovers to appeal to working folks and young people like him.

Not Pocket Books. Heaven forbid!

No, Epstein explained, he envisioned a larger format and better paper, the size and guts of hardbacks, but with paper covers—quality products costing more than Pocket Books but less than hardcovers. The owners were intrigued. That conversation launched "quality" or "trade" paperbacks, the first softcover books sold in bookshops. Epstein called his Doubleday imprint Anchor Books and released his first list in 1953 at the tender age of twenty-three. Trade paperbacks were an immediate hit. Today it's impossible to imagine publishing without them—witness this book.

Trade paperbacks fueled a bookstore bonanza. Two groups loved the new format: adult readers who wanted to stretch their book dollars, and the huge baby boom generation, whose seventy million members were starting to buy books and had no prejudice against paperbacks.

The book boom also created more space for indie presses, notably one with a bohemian, avant-garde edge, Grove Press (now Grove Atlantic). Founded in 1947, Grove soon was publishing Albert Camus, Lawrence Ferlinghetti, Bertolt Brecht, Kerouac, and Ginsberg. The house was also indicted on obscenity charges for publishing unexpurgated editions of D. H. Lawrence's *Lady Chatterley's Lover*, Henry Miller's *Tropic of Cancer*, and William Burrough's *Naked Lunch*. Grove's publisher, Barney Rosset (1922–2012), went to trial at great expense and prevailed in all three. Those cases played a pivotal role in ending literary censorship in the United States and made Rosset a hero to advocates for freedom of expression.

Throughout the 1950s, publishers and booksellers enjoyed soaring sales. Then, during the 1960s, sales exploded, almost *quadrupling*. Publishers rushed record numbers of titles into print: in 1959, 14,876, and by 1969, more than twice that, 29,579, which prompted the *New Yorker* writer Joseph Mitchell (1908–1996) to resurrect an old lament: "If there was anything the human race had a sufficiency of, a sufficiency and a surfeit, it was books. When I thought of the cataracts of books, the Niagaras of books, the rushing rivers of books, the oceans of books, the tons and truckloads and trainloads of books . . . , only a very few of which would be worth picking up and looking at, let alone reading."

In addition, a record number of entrepreneurs decided that what the world needed was another independent bookstore. Membership in the American Booksellers Association rose steadily from 1,200 in 1955 to 5,500 in 1995, including Lawrence Ferlinghetti's City Lights in San Francisco, California (founded in 1953), Tattered Cover in Denver, Colorado (1971), Powell's in Portland, Oregon (1971, the world's largest indie bookseller), and Skylight Books in Los Angeles (1996). But even as publishers and booksellers hit the jackpot, they fretted that paperbacks might destroy the great engine that had always powered publishing, hardcover books.

The Big Fear: Would Paperbacks Kill Hardcovers?

After trade paperbacks appeared, how did publishers keep selling hardcover books? They published books in hardcover, then waited at least a year to release them in paperback. But how many books must be read immediately? And if they absolutely had to be, they could be found in libraries. Otherwise, why not wait for the cheaper trade paperback? Or the even cheaper mass-market edition?

Every time consumers opted for paperbacks over hardbacks, their decisions hit publishers, booksellers, and authors in the wallet. Book people saw only one way to recoup the loss: volume and plenty of it, selling mountains of books in all formats from morning to night.

That's exactly what happened. During the 1960s, books sold as never before. Better yet, publishers of bestsellers discovered a new way to hit the jackpot: auctions of mass-market rights. In the 1950s, bestsellers' mass-market rights sold for around $10,000. In the '60s, some netted six figures, and by the '70s, millions.

Even so, in the 1960s, the University of Chicago professor Edward Shils (1910–1995) declared bookselling endangered, asserting that Americans showed little interest in reading. And in 1966, the media analyst Marshall McLuhan said, "Clotheslines, seams in stockings, and books—all are obsolete." Yet during the 1960s, despite the lure of movies, television, and transistor radios, baby boomers became history's largest generation of readers, and book sales reached heights previously unimagined.

Suburbs, Malls, and "the Chains" Change Publishing

Although PR pioneer Edward Bernays failed to dissuade Depression-era book borrowing, another of his ideas bore juicy fruit. He urged publishers to encourage builders to add something novel to new homes: built-in bookshelves. Bernays figured that homebuyers would fill them—which they did, during the post–World War II explosion of suburbs—and thanks to Epstein and Pocket Books, they were not above filling them with paperbacks.

But where did literary suburbanites go for books? Until the 1960s, independent booksellers inhabited small, funky, cluttered shops off the beaten track. This made perfect sense. Bookselling was a low-volume, low-profit business best suited to low-rent locations. But after the war, bookselling changed, which transformed publishing. The middle class moved to the suburbs, where they found not historical retail districts with perhaps a little bookshop down a side street, but enormous shopping malls anchored by department stores.

Starting around 1960, mall-based department stores faced a strategic dilemma: What to do about books? Eighty years earlier, the first department stores had embraced bookselling to capitalize on their cachet with upscale shoppers. In the 1960s, department stores in the new malls began turning their book departments into freestanding bookstores for the same reason, to add class to suburban shopping centers.

Walden Book Company went from renting books during the Depression to selling them after World War II. Renamed Walden Books (later Waldenbooks), in 1962, the company opened its first store in a suburban Pittsburgh mall and soon expanded to others, becoming the first chain bookseller.

Executives of the Dayton Company, a Minneapolis-based department store firm (now Target), watched closely. They liked Walden's model, and in 1966, at a mall in Edina, Minnesota, they opened the first B. Dalton Bookseller. Over the next decade, other chains appeared, among them Scribner's, Pickwick, Crown, and the two that became dominant: Borders, launched in 1971 in Ann Arbor, Michigan, as an antiquarian bookshop, and Barnes & Noble, founded in 1917 in New York City and now owned by Elliott Management, which also owns the Waterstones bookstore chain in the UK. By the early 1980s, department stores had departed the book business, and most malls boasted stand-alone bookstores, overwhelmingly chain outlets.

For independent booksellers, competition from department store book sections had been bad enough. Now the independents' rivals weren't little nooks up the escalator but full-fledged stores with high-visibility sidewalk frontage, huge display windows, and more titles than ever. In addition, the chains' many outlets, huge volume, and centralized ordering gave them unprecedented leverage. Crown negotiated eye-popping wholesale discounts, then offered deeper-than-ever retail discounts, snatching market share from the indies and driving many out of business.

By the 1970s, a militant faction of the American Booksellers Association pressed the organization to sue the chains for antitrust violations. Other ABA members feared the high cost of litigation and the real possibility of losing. The controversy simmered for a decade, then boiled over in 1982, when a breakaway faction, the Northern California Booksellers Association (NCBA), sued several majors for granting the chains preferential discounts. The ABA eventually joined the suit. Publishers retorted that standard business practices granted discounts based on order size. The independents placed small orders and got the standard discount. The chains placed much larger orders and received larger discounts. *What's wrong with that?*

In 1986, after four years of litigation, a judge ruled in favor of the NCBA, not because of preferential discounts, but because publishers had granted them in secret. The publishers appealed. The case dragged on another decade. In 1996, the publishers finally settled, agreeing to end secret discounts. But the independents' victory was Pyrrhic. By the time the suit settled, ABA membership had declined from 5,500 members to 3,200, a drop of 42 percent.

Meanwhile, the chains continued to grow, spread, and merge. Eventually, both Waldenbooks and B. Dalton disappeared, and by the 1990s, Borders and Barnes & Noble together accounted for 43 percent of trade sales, approximately the share Amazon claims today, with the independents selling around 20 percent.

Jason Epstein ultimately left Doubleday for Random House, where he was editorial director for decades. In 1962, New York newspapers went on strike. Epstein was appalled that for its duration, no book reviews would be published in the nation's book capital. So he, his wife, and two friends launched the *New York Review of Books*. They considered it a temporary stopgap publication, but when the strike ended, the *New York Review* continued to publish. Today its circulation tops one hundred thousand.

18

The Bumpy Road to Blockbusters, as Books' Shelf Life Falls to "Somewhere between Milk and Yogurt"

The arrival of trade paperbacks continued books' transformation from rare luxuries to totems of affluence to just another box of Minute Rice (introduced in the 1940s). Television was fast becoming the nation's dominant mass medium, and executives of the Ford Foundation decided that its programming should include the voices of the intelligentsia. The Ford Foundation sponsored a show, *Omnibus* (1952–1961), whose mission was to "raise the level" of entertainment. *Omnibus* featured interviews with many highbrow authors. Publishers could not afford to advertise on television, but thanks to *Omnibus*, some top authors reached the broadcast audience at no cost to publishers—and sold tons of books. As sales boomed and books and authors became fixtures of newspapers, magazines, radio, and even TV, publishers coined money as never before.

Unfortunately for publishers, the silver cloud of the 1960s sales boom had dark linings:

• Bestselling authors' advances soared. Some of their titles didn't earn out, saddling their publishers with huge losses.

•The bookstore explosion forced publishers to print, warehouse, and ship more copies than ever, plus field larger sales forces, raising their costs considerably.

•Distribution continued to be exasperating. Starting in the 1950s, shipping migrated to the new Interstate Highway System, but books were still heavy and trucking companies charged top dollar.

•Wholesalers were slow to pay or went bankrupt. When they failed, publishers got pennies on the dollar, if anything.

•As titles proliferated and bookstores grew larger, book placement on "first-look" front tables became increasingly valuable. Booksellers, especially the chains, demanded that publishers pay for it—as much as $10,000 per title for front-table spots chain-wide.

•Finally, more than one-third of books boomeranged as returns for full credit: 35 percent of hardcovers, 23 percent of trade paperbacks, and 47 percent of mass-market titles.

Unit costs, or cost per copy, had never been lower, but publishers' total cost of doing business rose inexorably. Many majors experienced serious cash crunches. Some went under. But before pulling the plug, many merged with—actually, were absorbed by—financially stronger houses. In fire sales, they sold their two assets, their names and backlists, becoming imprints, wholly owned subsidiaries. Their names still appeared on the spines of books, but they were no longer autonomous enterprises.

For the absorbers, bulking up had two advantages. They could unload staff, which reduced overhead. Of course, this forced surviving employees to work harder and handle more titles. In addition, surviving publishers acquired houses' backlists cheap, enabling them to sell modest numbers of ever-more books for years, which helped keep the lights on.

From the 1960s into the 1980s, publishing houses inked three hundred mergers. Random House bought Knopf, then Ballantine. Harper & Row acquired Basic Books and then Lippincott. Doubleday bought Dial and Delacorte . . . and on and on. But merging beat the wolf back from the door only so far.

Publishers needed financing to compete in the increasingly brutal book business. Meanwhile, some had become wealthy, and their social circles included New York bankers. They approached their buddies for loans, but the vaults remained firmly shut.

Bankers: *You have no real collateral—no factories, real estate, oil rigs, or truck fleets. Your only real asset is your staff, but every night, they walk out the door.*

Publishers: *Wait! What about our backlists?*

Bankers: *You want us to lend you millions based on future sales of* Gone with the Wind? *Dream on.*

The majors considered the bankers myopic. Backlists had been solid gold ever since Modern Library launched Random House. But the money-men saw things differently and wouldn't budge.

Meanwhile, chain booksellers suddenly made a new demand: more bestsellers. For centuries, publishers had presented their lists and booksellers had meekly marketed them. Now the chains pressured publishers for a steady stream of chartbusters that would fly off the shelves. Of course, publishers loved bestsellers, but they viewed them as happy accidents. Publishers couldn't believe booksellers were demanding a flood of them.

Why the sudden craving for huge sellers? Because bookshops were no longer backstreet boutiques. Mall bookstores occupied high-rent real estate, and there was only one way to pay the landlord: move tons of product day and night. Chain-store buyers were happy to stock titles that sold a half dozen copies a year, but to support their overhead, they needed a steady stream of titles that sold thousands. They needed a parade of super-bestsellers—*blockbusters*.

Big-Name Authors Gain Leverage

From 1900 through World War II, relations between publishers and agents remained chilly. But after the war, publishers realized that their erstwhile adversaries often had more bark than bite. Oh, sure, agents had forced them to sign contracts and pay advances. But in practice, almost all contracts favored publishers. Agents and the Authors Guild had failed to win accounting transparency and an industry-wide contract and royalty statement. And only bestselling authors could afford audits. For everyone else, publishers' records remained as opaque as obsidian. Publishers' antipathy toward agents softened. By 1970, the majors realized that agents actually saved them time and money.

• Agents became first readers, gatekeepers for the gatekeepers. Their efforts minimized publishers' cost of dealing with unsolicited manuscripts, the "slush pile" that arrived "over the transom."

• They introduced authors to publishers' worldview. When publishers dangled low offers, agents explained that only 10 percent of books made money, so publishers were cautious.

• Agents helped publishers police authors, leaning on those who missed delivery dates or refused revision requests.

• Best of all, agents were free. Authors paid them.

The chumminess ended in 1972, when Morton Janklow (1930–2022) got a call from his old friend William Safire (1929–2009). Janklow was a New York corporate lawyer, Safire a White House speechwriter and, later, *New York Times* columnist. Safire hoped to write a book about his boss, Richard Nixon, and asked Janklow to represent him. Janklow knew nothing about book publishing, but he had an acquaintance who worked for a major and asked to see the house's contract. A few days later, he asked his acquaintance, "Does any right-minded author sign this agreement?"

"Everyone signs. What don't you like about it?"

"Almost everything."

In contrast to other agents, Janklow took a hard line and won Safire an unusually large advance. Bestselling authors flocked to him. Janklow was also one of the first agents to auction book proposals (more shortly) and to raise his commission to 15 percent. Today, his firm, Janklow & Nesbit ranks among the world's largest literary agencies.

Another combative agent was Andrew Wylie (1947–). The son of a former Houghton Mifflin editor in chief, he riled publishers by treating them as the enemy and enraged other agents by attacking the collegiality of the agent-publisher relationship. Agents, he charged, "were basically in bed with the publishers, and these people over here, the writers, . . . [they were] children. . . . I came across jaw-dropping examples of agencies feeling a primary fealty to the publishing companies. And what I realized, which at the time was revolutionary, was that I was employed by the writer." Wylie wound up representing many big names and won them huge advances.

The new militants introduced a fresh moneymaker for big-name authors: book auctions. Before auctions, agents had quietly circulated proposals, hoping for the best. In contrast, auctions were catfights that forced publishers to bid directly against one another. If "auction fever" struck, it often became contagious—and advances soared. It's an old story: nobody wants you until somebody wants you, then everybody wants you. (Only one of my titles attracted more than one offer. During its auction, the initial bid *doubled*.)

Janklow and Wylie also rewrote contracts' "acceptability" clause. Previously, publishers could reject manuscripts for any reason. The new breed insisted that publishers provide cogent critiques with clear directions for revisions and extended deadlines to get the job done. The author-friendlier acceptability clause quickly became standard.

By the 1970s, the tiny proportion of authors who populated best-seller lists could make $1 million from a single book, netting their agents $150,000. Top agents became celebrities, and publishing changed as big-name authors gained something new: real leverage over publishers.

By the mid-1970s, the majors felt they were sailing between Scylla and Charybdis. Jason Epstein: "The excessive royalty guarantees demanded by the authors of predictable best-sellers render their profitability problematic, while the profitability of books in the broader category is made problematic by the unpredictability of their sales."

By the 1970s, the balance of power shifted. Publishers now found themselves beset by booksellers' demands for blockbusters and agents' demands for huge advances that increased the risk of publishing even the most bankable authors. Suddenly, top authors were calling the shots.

Meanwhile, the industry's laser focus on blockbusters stressed many publishers and dimmed the lights for most authors. Mergers increased. Median advances stalled, then started to fall.

The Blockbuster Era:
Publishers Throw Themselves at Media Conglomerates

The phrase "blockbuster era" dates from the *New Yorker*'s 1980 publication of "The Blockbuster Complex," by Thomas Whiteside (1918–1997). The article, and subsequent book, made headlines and deeply offended bibliophiles. Whiteside charged that the book business had been hijacked by international media conglomerates in a cultural coup d'état, much to the detriment of books, reading, and publishing's historical quirkiness. Whiteside's allegations quickly became a mantra: *Corporate ownership is ruining publishing.*

Corporate capitalism is certainly open to criticism. However, Whiteside got it backward. Media conglomerates didn't seize control of publishing. It was the other way around. The major publishers genuflected before the media giants. They needed capital to compete for blockbusters and couldn't get it any other way.

As one publisher told Whiteside, "When Frederick Forsyth's book *The Day of the Jackal* was published, in 1971, he got about a ten-thousand-dollar advance. For his second Viking book, *The Odessa File* [1972], he got a half-million-dollar advance, and for his most recent book, *The Devil's Alternative* [1979], he got an advance not far from two million dollars. Soon, with the huge escalation in advances being demanded by writers and their agents, we found we had reached the point where we could not conduct business [with] available cash."

Mergers didn't solve the problem and banks wouldn't lend, which left only one alternative. Starting in the late 1960s, CBS acquired Holt, MCA bought Putnam, Gulf + Western Industries absorbed Simon & Schuster and Prentice Hall, and on and on. Today, four international media conglomerates and one private equity firm own all major American publishers.

Whiteside flailed publishers for "capitulating" to the conglomerates, but contrary to his own thesis, he found no evidence of ruin: "There have been widespread fears that conglomerate control of publishing houses will result in some kind of censorship or backstage blacklisting of books critical of or abhorrent to the political or economic outlook of the conglomerates concerned. . . . I have come across no evidence of it." Fears of incipient conglomerate political censorship appeared unfounded.

Today, four decades after the majors threw themselves at the media conglomerates, hand-wringing over their ruination appears silly. In 1980, the year Whiteside's book appeared, U.S. publishers released 42,377 titles. Today, with indie-press releases and self-published e-books, it's 2.7 million, sixty-six times as many. Corporate ownership certainly hasn't stifled output.

Have the conglomerates shunned literary fiction? Advocates for highbrow novels insist they have, that the conglomerates care only about the bottom line and don't publish fiction that's not clearly commercial. But from the moment the first book business evolved into the second, bibliophiles accused pre-conglomerate publishers of the same sin.

Have the conglomerates muzzled anyone for political reasons? Not that I can see. Visit, say, HarperCollins.com and scan the catalogue. As I write, its list contains several books espousing leftist views. Meanwhile, the house is owned by Rupert Murdoch, a staunch conservative.

If corporate executives nix titles as noncommercial or for political reasons, university presses and the many indie publishers provide good alternatives. And authors can self-publish anything.

Whiteside argued that conglomerate ownership of publishers might have *decreased* censorship. Entrepreneurial publishers rejected manuscripts for all sorts of discriminatory reasons, including authors' politics, race, gender, and religion.

One example: In 1925, editor Max Perkins showed his boss, Charles Scribner, the manuscript of Bruce Barton's *The Man Nobody Knows*, which portrayed Jesus as a super-salesman. Scribner rejected it as blasphemous. Published by another house, it was a bestseller. Scribner remembered the book and confronted Perkins about its rejection. Perkins reminded the boss of his religious objections. Scribner replied, "But, Mr. Perkins, you didn't tell me it would sell four hundred thousand copies."

The jaw-dropping sums required to throw the dice on potential blockbusters gave the book business an air of unreality. "With all the conglomerate money in publishing today," said former Ballantine president Ronald Busch (1928–1987), "it was like playing Monopoly. If we had to use our own resources, we would have thought twice about bidding as much as we did. . . . But with a parent conglomerate that has annual sales of two billion dollars and up, and two or three million shareholders, what is the risk? If you are wrong, the stockholders don't feel it."

Bibliophiles demonized corporate publishing: *All corporations care about is money.* That's true, of course, but it was nothing new. The corporate commitment to the bottom line actually argued *against* censorship. If authors could muster audiences to buy their work, publishers were happy to release it. Most publishers are largely indifferent to what books *say* as long as they *sell*.

In 1970, a friend of mine attended a party whose guests included the 1960s anti–Vietnam War activist Abbie Hoffman (1936–1989).

He'd just completed a book manuscript and wondered what everyone thought of his working title. A majority, my friend included, insisted the publisher would never use it. "Why not?" Hoffman countered. "It'll sell books." The publisher loved Hoffman's title, *Steal This Book* (1971).

The transition from entrepreneurial to corporate publishing has neither limited book buyers' choices nor instigated censorship. However, among publishing employees, it caused great suffering. The book business became more bureaucratic and alienating. Informal chats at watercoolers morphed into formal memos to distant bureaucrats. Downsizing also took a toll. I knew several editors who got fired after conglomerates absorbed their houses. But in an enterprise that's always been tough for everyone all the time, it was business as usual.

Copy Machine Piracy: Publishers Sue Kinko's

After defining the first book business, during the second, piracy declined, though international copyright treaties had almost nothing to do with it. The driver was the economics of printing. As industrial publishing matured, pirates had to crank up industrial presses, which required substantial investment and, in turn, discouraged piracy—until 1959.

That was the year Xerox introduced its first photocopier. Copy machines quickly became ubiquitous, and once again, piracy became cheap and easy. People copied everything like crazy.

In 1962, a Baltimore medical publisher, Williams & Wilkins (now Lippincott Williams & Wilkins), sued the Department of Health, Education, and Welfare (HEW, now the Department of Health and Human Services), charging that the agency's rampant photocopying of the company's research journals infringed its copyrights. The case lasted a decade. In 1972, the court ruled in favor of the publisher—and raised a ruckus in medical education.

HEW: *How can we train doctors if they can't copy journal articles?*

W&W: *You trained them just fine before photocopiers.*

HEW: *What do you want?*

W&W: *Buy reprint rights from us.*

HEW: *But it's only piracy if someone* sells *copies. Students are copying for personal use. That's fair use.*

W&W: *Perhaps, but personal copying invites commercial piracy.*

Outraged by W&W's insistence on licensing fees, some medical centers boycotted the company's journals. In 1973, the government appealed and won. The company appealed to the U.S. Supreme Court, where one justice recused himself, resulting in a 4–4 tie. The lower court ruling held. It legalized unrestrained photocopying of copyrighted material.

Photocopying piracy quickly became popular on college campuses. Professors and students had long complained that required texts produced captive audiences, which allowed publishers to charge fortunes. (My children attended college from 2004 to 2012. Their textbooks averaged $500 per semester.) To save students money, professors pulled material from several sources and printed their own course anthologies at copy shops, often Kinko's (since 2008, FedEx).

In 1989, eight publishers sued Kinko's for copyright infringement. The publishers documented widespread duplication and argued it exceeded fair use. In 1991, the federal court ruled that while students could copy small portions of copyrighted works for personal use, Kinko's had illegally profited by printing thousands of college-course anthologies without paying a dime for rights. Kinko's paid $2 million in damages.

As part of the settlement, the parties agreed to affiliate with the Copyright Clearance Center in Danvers, Massachusetts, which licenses reproduction of copyrighted material. Since 1978, the center has distributed over $1.3 billion to publishers.

"Somewhere between Milk and Yogurt"

As chain bookstores proliferated, releases set records—in 1970, thirty-six thousand; in 1980, forty-two thousand. Competition intensified for top authors, reviews, shelf space, promotional opportunities, and readers. As a result, books lost shelf life.

From the 1950s into the 1970s, books had around six months to catch on, or in publisher parlance, "find an audience." But as booksellers' attention increasingly focused on blockbusters, the window began to close. The chains quickly distinguished sales leaders from laggards. Suddenly, books no longer had six months. The chains started returning copies after five months, then four, then three. Publishers reeled, but what could they do? When titles didn't sell briskly, mall booksellers returned them with a vengeance—and a grim joke made the rounds. The shelf life of new titles had fallen to "somewhere between milk and yogurt."

Sales Become Increasingly Bimodal

Uncle Tom's Cabin inaugurated the great divide: bestseller or not. Bestseller lists and the popularity effect sharpened the distinction. And by the 1980s, as new releases topped forty thousand a year, the mass media lavished attention on an ever-smaller proportion of them.

Consequently, from 1986 to 1996, bestsellers' share of trade sales doubled, and of the top hundred bestselling novels, almost two-thirds (63 percent) were written by just six authors: Tom Clancy, John Grisham, Stephen King, Dean Koontz, Michael Crichton, and Danielle Steel.

Today, book sales have become even more bimodal. *Fifty Shades of Grey* has sold 150 million copies, while only 6 percent of titles sell one thousand, and four out of five self-published titles don't sell one hundred. Most authors are to the big names what garage bands are to the Rolling Stones.

Is this healthy? Hard to say. There's no shortage of good to great books out there. My to-be-read stack is a tower. But with so much attention focused on so few titles, many excellent books get ignored, robbing readers of the opportunity to discover them and leaving their authors frustrated or worse.

= 19 =

BookScan and (Non)Transparency in Publishing

When publishers discovered that hyping strong sales could build buzz, they systematically exaggerated all sales figures. During the 1990s, my agent had lunch with an editor at a major who had high hopes for a new title. "Our release just announced a first printing of twenty-five thousand," he proclaimed, then added sotto voce, "We're actually printing eight thousand."

Such dissembling became difficult after 2001, when Nielsen launched BookScan, which claims to track 85 percent of trade book sales. Initially, publishers recoiled. Auditing meant they could no longer exaggerate. But BookScan audited everyone so no one could fib. And if the world finally learned that only a thimbleful of titles sells more than a few thousand copies, so be it. (Today BookScan is owned by the NPD Group in the United States and by Nielsen elsewhere.)

But the world never learned. BookScan information is available only to subscribers. When the service debuted, subscriptions started at $2,500 a year, well beyond most authors' means.

BookScan throttled most authors and agents. Suddenly, publishers knew the sales of every book, not just their own. They told agents, *Your authors are worth only as much as their previous titles' sales.* Say a book sold two thousand copies in its $25 hardcover edition (at 10 percent, royalties of $5,000) and ten thousand as a $20 trade paperback (at 8 percent, $16,000), total income $21,000. Before BookScan, a wily agent with a strong proposal for a subsequent title might have negotiated a big advance. But armed with BookScan data, publishers said, *Her last one earned twenty-one grand. We won't pay a dime more for her next.*

Publishers downplay BookScan, noting that it's just one of many factors in decisions about acquisitions and advances. Perhaps. But would you renew an expensive annual BookScan subscription if it didn't pay off? BookScan has paid off handsomely by reducing advances for non-bestselling authors. Ask any agent. According to the *New Yorker*, since BookScan debuted, advances have declined at least 25 percent.

Incidentally, Amazon provides authors with free BookScan information for their own titles. Set up an Author Central page and click "Reports + Marketing," then scroll down to "BookScan Weekly Sales Report." If your sales figures don't appear, contact the Authors Guild. AG staff helped me get my BookScan numbers.

How Accurate Is BookScan?

BookScan claims to track 85 percent of trade sales, but publishers and self-publishers insist it comes nowhere near that. One publisher told me: "One of our top-selling books has sold more than one hundred thousand copies, but BookScan says it's sold only half that number."

Self-publishers complain that BookScan largely ignores them. For example, the service overlooks specialty stores. If your dog-training guide sells mostly in pet shops, those sales don't register. Nor does BookScan track back-of-the-room sales after appearances, significant for some authors. In addition, BookScan doesn't count sales at Walmart, Sam's Club, Costco, drugstores, and supermarkets.

Like bestseller lists, BookScan has never revealed its methodology, so it's anyone's guess how accurate the service's numbers are. But when BookScan underreports sales, publishers benefit and authors lose. Mistakenly low sales figures depress advances for authors' subsequent titles, which cuts publishers' costs.

Late Twentieth-Century Piracy:
"Ten Percent or It's Out of Print"

During the late twentieth century, contracts for hardcovers typically included royalty escalators: 10 percent for the first five thousand copies, 12.5 percent for the second five thousand, then 15 percent. The escalator rewarded authors for titles that sold well and acknowledged that, over time, publishers' costs decline. Advances, editing, production, and promotion are all one-time front-end expenses. As those costs get paid off, there's a larger pie to split. At least in theory.

One of my books sold out its first printing, moving me up to 12.5 percent—or so I thought, until my agent opened a letter from the publisher. It acknowledged that my royalty should increase, but alas, the poor company could not afford to honor the escalator clause. The publisher offered me a choice: agree to continuing at 10 percent or the company would take the book out of print.

My agent protested, but the house wouldn't budge. *Ten percent or kiss it goodbye.*

I called a lawyer, who said, "Any first-year law student can tell you that contracts don't obligate anyone to anything. They're simply evidence of previous agreements. They don't mean the parties still agree. Contracts get renegotiated all the time. Your publisher is renegotiating yours."

"But we're *not* negotiating," I sputtered. "It's extortion."

"Sure, but contracts are only as strong as the will to enforce them. To enforce yours, you'd have to sue. Do you want to spend years and a ton of money in litigation?"

I stamped around the house for a few days, then signed for 10 percent. The difference between the two royalty rates was sixty-three cents per copy. At the time, the publisher, a New York major, had revenue in the tens of millions.

Subsequently, that book sold out its second printing, and I should have ridden the escalator to 15 percent. My agent received another letter. Alas, the poor publisher . . .

My agent replied, *If you can't go 15 percent, how about 12.5? That's what you should have paid on the five thousand copies sold since the last time you reamed my client.*

The publisher hemmed and hawed, then finally acquiesced.

That book ultimately sold twenty thousand in hardback, but on fifteen thousand of them, I was extorted into relinquishing sixty-three cents a copy. The publisher made an extra $9,450 ($28,000 today).

I could name the house, but that would allow other publishers to call the offender a bad apple. It's not about bad apples. It's about a business model that steps on those who have no leverage.

Wait, Who Wrote This?

In 1987, I wrote a little book on preventing and treating colds and flu. Some years after it appeared, a librarian friend mentioned that a publisher had sent her a bound galley of a new book on the subject, and would I like to see it?

A few paragraphs in, I thought, *This sounds familiar.* I quickly realized that the new book was actually my book re-titled and with someone else's name on the cover. The pirate, a Connecticut woman, had copied almost the entire text verbatim.

The Authors Guild referred me to a lawyer.

"Happens all the time," he said. "She probably got a contract for very little money. She did some research but never got around to writing the thing. As her deadline loomed, she copied the best source. In a way, you should feel flattered."

I felt anything but and wanted to sue.

He asked, "Where in Connecticut does she live?" By chance, he'd grown up near Hartford. When I mentioned the town, he said, "Too bad. Lower middle class."

"Meaning?"

"That she probably doesn't have enough assets to be worth suing. I'd be happy to represent you, but you'd have to put up a big retainer. The litigation would take years. And it would cost way more than you'd ever recover. My advice: Let it go."

I tried but couldn't. Perhaps there was another way . . .

I wrote the thief a letter and copied her agent: *Picture me sending your book and mine to your publisher. I'm confident your contract requires submission of an original work. Yours isn't. Your publisher will undoubtedly cancel your contract for fraud, not release the book, and demand the return of your advance. In addition, picture me sending your book and mine to the* Hartford Courant, New York Times, Boston Globe, *and every TV and radio station within fifty miles of you. You'll have satellite trucks camped out at your door, and what will the neighbors think? You have two choices: public humiliation or a generous offer. You have seventy-two hours before I go to FedEx.*

The pirate's agent fell all over himself apologizing. "She got next to nothing and copied the best source."

"How much was 'next to nothing'?"

The amount was, indeed, paltry, but she didn't earn it. I did.

"Okay. I want a letter of apology, a copy of the contract proving the advance, a check for the full amount, and coauthor credit."

The agent begged for mercy. *She can hardly pay her rent.* I have a soft spot for writers even when they're crooks, so I settled for credit and half the money.

Today, with digital publishing and millions of new releases annually, what's the chance of plagiarists getting caught? I discovered mine totally by accident. The book business was founded on piracy—and today it's easier than ever.

In 2023, the *Los Angeles Times* discovered ninety-five instances of plagiarism in *The Book of Animal Secrets*, by Dr. David Agus, a medical expert for CBS and a professor at the University of Southern California. The publisher withdrew it "until a fully revised and corrected edition can be released."

For coverage of contemporary plagiarism, visit PlagiarismToday.com.

Dude, Where's My $500?

In 1978, I wrote my first book in longhand on yellow pads. I revised as I typed it, then marked up the typescript, retyped, and sent the publisher a ream of paper. The house paid for typesetting, which at the time cost $1,200 (around $3,500 today).

A few years later, for my second book, instead of a typescript, I sent a floppy disk. The text could be converted into type electronically for around $200, saving the publisher $1,000. That year, American publishers released forty-five thousand titles. If every author submitted a disk and publishers paid $200 per conversion instead of $1,200 for typesetting, they would have saved $45 million ($140 million today).

Agents and the Authors Guild argued that writers should share in the savings. *Let's split it. If authors submit disks, how about reimbursing them $500 per title?*

But publishing continued to be brutal, and the vast majority of authors continued to have little leverage. The digital-typesetting windfall went entirely to publishers. Authors received nothing.

As the digital revolution developed, no single event marked the end of the second book business. But for me, publishers' refusal to share digital-typesetting savings crystalized the transition. From the moment the second book business began yielding to the third, publishers felt an existential threat. Many houses failed or were forced into mergers. Surviving publishers worked overtime to preserve and bolster publisher-centrism—often at the expense of non-bestselling authors, the 99.99+ percent. Feeling up against the wall rarely produces generosity.

Forward into the Past

As we've seen, the first and second book businesses offered important advantages over prehistoric campfire tales. Books fixed stories exactly as written. And as cultures grew, no individual could remember every-thing, but books collected in libraries came close.

However, publishing also imposed one key disadvantage. Informa-tion no longer flowed directly from authors to audiences. As printing developed, storytelling had more to do with the intermediaries than the creators.

The third book business, digital publishing, debuted with a grand promise: elimination of "gatekeepers," authors communicating directly with readers. That promise has been fulfilled in spades for some authors of genre fiction. But for the rest of us, the third book business has made the writing life considerably more challenging—and usually much less lucrative.

Part III

The Third Book Business
Digital Publishing From the Millennium to...

20

Brave New (Digital) World

In Shakespeare's *The Tempest*, shipwrecked Miranda has grown up on an uncharted island isolated from all humanity except for her father. Then a ship founders. Miranda meets the wreck's survivors, her first encounter with other people. She feels overwhelmed with joy: "How beauteous mankind is! O brave new world, / That has such people in't!" But in his 1932 dystopian novel, *Brave New World*, Aldous Huxley (1894–1963) transformed the phrase from a celebration into an alarm warning that powerful new technologies might overwhelm humanity. Celebration or alarm? The third book business involves elements of both. It has opened up tremendous new possibilities for books and reading, while also threatening everyone in the book business, leaving most authors feeling more confounded than ever.

Scribes yielded to Gutenberg because printing presses allowed fewer people to produce more copies of more books faster and cheaper. During the industrial revolution, hand-operated printing presses yielded to their higher-speed industrial descendants for the same reason. The digital revolution has taken this progression close to its technological limit. Digital publishing now allows one lone individual to publish an infinite number of copies of e-books in the blink of an eye for next to nothing and distribute them worldwide almost for free.

Back in the 1960s, William Targ (1907–1999), then editor in chief at G. P. Putnam's Sons, said, "The trouble with the publishing business is that too many people who have half a mind to write a book do so." If he only knew.

The third book business has produced more new releases, both print and e-books, than anyone ever imagined possible. Books have multiplied like the brooms in *Fantasia*'s "The Sorcerer's Apprentice" scene. Since 2000, the U.S. population has increased 20 percent, but new releases have rocketed forty-fold, 4,000 percent.

In 2021, publishing houses released 395,000 new titles. Self-publishers added 2.3 million. That year's total, 2.7 million books, meant approximately 7,400 releases every day, 308 per hour, 5 every minute. Put another way, during the entire twentieth century, U.S. publishers released an estimated 2.5 million titles. Since the millennium, that many new books have appeared *every year or two*.

When Did the Second Book Business Become the Third?

That's fuzzy, but the decades-long shift from the first book business to the second provides perspective. Industrial printing debuted before the Civil War but didn't dominate book publishing until the 1880s. It takes time for new technologies to displace their predecessors. Meanwhile, in 1843, Ticknor & Fields became the first publisher to pay to print an American author. The house wanted to sign the big-name poet John Greenleaf Whittier (1807–1892) and offered the unheard-of perk to close the deal. But most authors continued to pay for printing for another seventy-five years, through World War I. So the transition from the first book business to the second took thirty years to germinate and seventy-five to flower.

Similarly, the transition from industrial to digital publishing started long before e-books appeared. It began in 1966, when an English bookseller, W. H. Smith, developed a computer-readable nine-digit book identification system, Standard Book Numbering (SBN). Ten-digit International Standard Book Numbers (ISBNs) debuted in 1970, and since 2007, they have contained thirteen digits. (Universal product codes, the bar graphics on other consumer items, were envisioned in the 1940s but languished until ISBNs demonstrated their utility.)

Turning titles into a string of numbers was only the beginning. Next came computerized inventory management (c. 1975), followed by digital typesetting and word processing (c. 1980). These innovations shifted physical publishing onto the electronic desktop. Around the millennium, e-books appeared along with digital print-on-demand, which enabled cost-effective printing of small runs of physical books. These two developments allowed authors to self-publish their work without conventional publishers.

Jeff Bezos founded Amazon.com in 1994 as an online bookstore. In 2007, Amazon released its Kindle e-book reader. The same year, Amazon launched Kindle Direct Publishing, which allowed anyone to publish e-books quickly, easily, and super cheaply and distribute them electronically worldwide. In addition to e-books, Amazon was also happy to distribute print-on-demand titles.

So, the third book business germinated in the mid-1960s and flowered four decades later. That's about half the time it took the first book business to become the second. Which makes sense. Digital technology has accelerated the pace of change.

The digital revolution has transformed every industry, but particularly media enterprises whose product is information. Unlike socks or pineapples, with the right equipment, information can be dematerialized, transmitted electronically, and reconstituted anywhere. The implications for books have been profound:

• **More, faster, cheaper.** Benjamin Franklin once said, "A method should be discovered to print a few copies of a work as cheaply per copy as when many are printed." Digital publishing has granted his wish—and not just because of e-books. Printing has also become considerably more cost-efficient. For up to five hundred copies, print-on-demand can produce standard trade paperbacks in record time for less per copy than the cost of a cappuccino. For larger runs, digitized offset printing delivers books at the lowest unit cost ever.

• **Goodbye gatekeepers!** This has been a siren song to legions of authors frustrated by rejections from agents and publishers. Digital publishing has freed authors to self-publish cost-effectively, and Amazon is delighted to sell their books. Some self-publishers reinvent the wheel by doing everything themselves. But most contract with publishing services companies (PSCs), publishers for hire, now increasingly called "hybrid publishers." If authors are willing to pay, PSCs can produce books that appear indistinguishable from those released by the majors.

• **Books rarely go out of print.** During the late twentieth century, new releases had six to twelve months to find an audience. If not, publishers pulled them out of print, sending them to the graveyard. But in the third book business, all books have become digital files that require no warehousing. Digital files can be maintained forever at low cost.

Consequently, these days few books go out of print. If someone orders, the file can be printed and shipped. For authors, the downside of digital publishing is a flood of new releases that could swamp Noah's ark. But the upside is that authors can promote their books for as long as they have the time, energy, and money.

• **Tons of free books.** Since the millennium, books have become so plentiful that, forget selling them, they're increasingly difficult to *give away*. Consider Little Free Libraries. This nonprofit, launched in 2009, boasts 150,000 free public bookcases from coast to coast. The dozen in my neighborhood are always stuffed full. If you want a specific title, you have to buy it or borrow from a library. But if you just want something to read, freebies abound.

• **Median sales per title have plummeted.** A tiny fraction of books still sell a hundred thousand copies. But as new releases have soared, median sales have been sliced thinner than a bookmark (see chart). Since 2010, new releases have averaged 2.8 million a year, with books amassing annual sales of around 800 million copies. Divide the number of books sold by the number of new titles, and the average book sells only around 286 copies. But annual sales include both new releases and backlist titles. Factor in backlist sales, and the average new release sells even fewer. Of course, some titles sell huge numbers, which means that many sell next to none. The typical self-published book sells only around a hundred copies.

• **Authors' incomes fall.** With median sales way down, most authors' book incomes have fallen off a cliff. A 2022 Authors Guild survey shows that full-time authors' median annual income that year from all writing-related activities was $23,000, and from book writing alone, $12,000. For part-time authors—the vast majority of book writers—the figures were $8,500 and $2,800, respectively. In 2023, my royalty income from my eighteen books was $1,500. Compared with fifty years ago, book writing has become more of a hobby and less of a career.

Only 6 Percent of New Releases Sell One Thousand Copies

New releases: Copies sold	Percentage of new titles in that sales range
1-99	79%
100-999	16.9%
1,000-4,999	5.6%
5,000-49,999	1.9%
50,000-99,999	0.06% (6 in 10,000)
100,000-249,999	0.03% (3 in 10,000)
250,000-499,999	0.01% (1 in 10,000)
500,000-999,999	0.002% (2 in 100,000)
1,000,000+	0.001% (1 in 100,000)

(Greco et al. *The Culture and Commerce of Publishing in the 21st Century*, p. 212. Figures add up to more than 100 percent because of rounding.)

•**Agents have been hammered**. They earn 15 percent of less and less.

•**Publishers and booksellers have also suffered**. As mentioned, most self-published titles sell in two figures. Let's assume they sell fifty. With some two million self-releases annually, their sales total around one hundred million copies a year. Publishers and booksellers make nothing from those sales. Every time readers choose self-published titles over browsing at bookshops, publishers and booksellers lose money. Who makes the money? The self-publishing platforms and PSCs. Of course, they have every right to be in business and become successful. Some of their income comes from authors rejected by publishing houses, but some comes from authors who could have published with mainstream publishers but for whatever reason decided not to.

Some authors and publishers still prosper, and many of the new PSCs have too. But blue-sky predictions of authors triumphant in a world without gatekeepers have popped like soap bubbles.

Welcome to the third book business. The digital revolution has enabled authors to express themselves as never before—while pulling the financial rug out from under the vast majority of them and almost everyone else in publishing.

For most authors, writing books has always been a labor of love. Now that's truer than ever. Today, book writing is much more likely to *cost* authors money than *make* any.

The Book Business Digitally Transformed

Books published today look virtually indistinguishable from those released fifty years ago, but everything about their production has changed:

•**Composition.** Some fossils may still write longhand or use typewriters, but word processing is infinitely more efficient.

•**Editing.** Editors once jotted comments in manuscript margins or attached Post-it notes, then mailed photocopies to authors for review. Now they use Track Changes and email, which saves time, paper, copying, and postage.

•**Indexing.** In pre-digital times, a small army of freelancers, mostly stay-at-home moms, indexed books by hand for $500 to $1,000 per title ($1,500 to $3,000 today). Now with indexing software, anyone can create comprehensive indexes electronically faster for less.

• **Production.** No more pasting up pages with scissors and glue. Today designers produce print-ready pages on-screen and email them to printers. Or the final product is an e-book that's never printed.

• **Printing.** For more than one thousand copies, offset remains the most cost-effective option. But for smaller runs, digital print-on-demand delivers books remarkably cheap.

• **Distribution.** It's still a major headache. But tracking software shows where books are at any moment. And with e-books, warehousing and shipping are no longer necessary, which saves a fortune.

• **Returns.** During the twentieth century, books were printed then (hopefully) sold. But many didn't sell, which generated returns that had to be disposed of. These days, many books aren't printed until they're purchased, and e-books require no shipping at all. During the first and second book businesses, it was "print then sell." Now, increasingly, it's "sell then print" (or download).

• **Lower overhead.** Why lease office space and provide desks, benefits, and toilet paper when most employees can work from home on their own computers and deliver work electronically? Most employees prefer largely remote work.

• **More publishers.** The second book business was a manufacturing enterprise. But digital technology has reduced the need for manufacture—and, according to self-publishing advocates, publishers' very raison d'être. In the third book business, it's easier and cheaper than ever to publish books, but harder than ever to sell them. Small- and medium-size publishers are betting there's a sweet spot between the promise and peril. In 1970, there were an estimated three thousand indie publishers in the United States. By 2010, there were thousands more, most of them publishing services companies.

The Publishing Transformation Still Waiting to Happen: Racial Equity

As digital technology revolutionized the book business, one aspect of publishing has remained stubbornly unchanged: its centuries-old domination by white people. Back in 1995, the (white) writer James Ledbetter penned an article in the *Village Voice* titled "The Unbearable Whiteness of Publishing." He observed that the people who populated publishing looked nothing like the country where they lived. Fast-forward thirty years, and according to a 2021 report by PEN America, the nonprofit that advocates for free expression, the situation is largely unchanged. A 2019 survey shows that white people comprise 78 percent of publishing executives, 85 percent of editorial employees, 81 percent of sales personnel, and 74 percent of marketing and publicity people. Not to mention that 80 percent of agents and book reviewers are white.

Meanwhile, more than 40 percent of Americans and 25 percent of book readers are people of color. Since the mid-twentieth century, publishers have not exactly ignored them—consider James Baldwin, Toni Morrison, Angela Davis, and Ta-Nehisi Coates, among many others. And yet writers of color continue to have a disproportionately tough time getting published. A report from Penguin Random House showed that from 2019 to 2021, the house's authors were: 75 percent white, 7 percent Asian, 6 percent Black, 5 percent Hispanic, 2 percent Middle Eastern, and less than 1 percent Native American and Pacific Islander. Ranked by advances, these figures skew even whiter.

Today, publishers discuss racial equity more than ever, a welcome change. Since the 2013 killing of Trayvon Martin galvanized the rallying cry "Black Lives Matter," several people of color have ascended to top management positions at the Big Five and other houses. Publishers have also hired more editors of color, who have released more books by nonwhite authors. That's progress. But like all major U.S. industries, publishing still has a long way to go before its workforce and output reflect twenty-first-century America.

From Book Reviews to BookTok

In the third book business, traditional print book reviews have plummeted. In 1990, the typical Sunday *New York Times Book Review* section contained forty-four pages and fifty-five reviews. In 2023, it was about half that size—twenty-four pages, thirty-five reviews. Other newspapers have also curtailed book reviewing or eliminated it altogether. Ditto many magazines.

In addition, *New York Times* reviews lean heavily toward Big Five releases. I tallied the publishers of every title the *Times* reviewed during May 2023. That month, the Big Five accounted for two-thirds of reviews. Titles published by other houses have slim chances of *Times* reviews, and self-published books have next to none. *PW* reviews several hundred self-published titles per year—among millions of releases.

Since the 1960s, a point of pride among independent booksellers has been their occasional ability to shepherd new releases onto the bestseller list. That was the case with Jean Auel's *The Clan of the Cave Bear* (1980) and Alice Sebold's *The Lovely Bones* (2002). Indie booksellers touted them and they took off. But very few books become the darlings of booksellers, and even when they do, commercial success is by no means assured. Not to mention that, compared with 1995, in 2023, there were fewer than half as many indies. Consequently, these days we hear less about the value of independent booksellers' endorsements.

In the twenty-first century, where do most book reviews appear? On Amazon, Goodreads, BookBub, and other sites. But compared with legacy periodicals, most of those reviews are much less likely to generate buzz and sales. Goodreads sponsors giveaways that enable authors to send free copies to readers who request them. I've given away hundreds of copies of my books through Goodreads but haven't noticed any change in BookScan sales estimates or my Amazon rankings.

As book reviews fade from the legacy media, their importance to book buyers has waned. In 2021, *Publishers Weekly* asked a large group of book buyers what led to their most recent purchases. In order of importance: recommendations from friends, familiarity with the author, family word of mouth, and social media. Not print reviews.

Does Social Media Really Sell Books?

Publishers and pundits urge authors to be Google-able, to build websites and establish strong social media presences. Does this strategy sell books? Possibly, but don't bet on it.

Social media worked fantastically for John Locke (1951–), the first author to sell one million copies of a self-published e-book. A Kentucky real estate investor, Locke published his first spy novel in 2009. By 2011, his series had sold more than a million copies. How? He writes thrillers, the only genre other than romance fiction able to sell huge numbers of e-books. He sold his books on Amazon—cheap, for $2.99. He developed a series and touted his entire list to anyone who even glanced at any of them. He trumpeted his work relentlessly through blog posts and social media. And he used a pay-for-raves site to purchase more than three hundred phony five-star "reviews." He describes his strategy in *How I Sold 1 Million eBooks in 5 Months.*

Social media—Instagram, Facebook, YouTube, and BookTok (the book-oriented galaxy in the TikTok universe)—also worked wonders for the romance novelist Colleen Hoover, thanks to social media influencers, some of whom boast millions of followers. Influencers touted Hoover's work in a huge number of BookTok videos. Thanks to that deluge of word of mouth, sales of Hoover's 2016 novel, *It Ends with Us,* soared. Several of her books have ascended to the *New York Times* bestseller list. And in the acknowledgments of her novel *Reminders of Him* (2022), she credits BookTok.

On the other hand, social media didn't do much for the singing star Billie Eilish. Her autobiographical photo book received a million-dollar advance on the strength of her ninety-seven million Instagram followers. Eight months after its release, the book had sold sixty-four thousand copies—major numbers in the twenty-first century, but only a tiny fraction of what her publisher hoped (and paid) for. Only one Eilish follower in 1,500 bought the book. Her publisher took a bath.

While anyone is free to market books through BookTok and other social media, the authors most likely to benefit are the small fraction of those who write romance fiction and mystery/thriller. For everyone else, investing time and money in a robust social media presence is professionally necessary to look like a serious author, but far from sufficient to sell many books.

Before this book, my previous release was a 2021 sexuality guide. My tech consultant produced an attractive website ($3,000) and myriad posts on Facebook, Instagram, and BookTok ($300 per month). I promoted the book through my blog (180,000 views per month), my sexuality Q&A website (1,500 views per month), my Substack newsletter (two thousand subscribers), thirty-five podcasts, a dozen group Zoom calls, and the nation's largest sexuality organization (six thousand members). After three years, that book had sold three thousand copies—not bad for a new release in the twenty-first century. In fact, pretty good, in the top 5 percent of sales. But saturation social media posts have not produced miracles. Keep your expectations low. "The only reliable part about it [the connection between social media and book sales]," says Shannon DeVito, an executive with Barnes & Noble, "is that it's unreliable."

Review Bombing: Technology Boosts Deception

Since World War II, reviews have been considered more or less trustworthy until proven otherwise. Most reviewers are scrupulous and thoughtful. But digital technology has enabled publication of deceptive reviews on a scale never previously imagined. And a new phrase has entered the lexicon: "review bombing," organized pans.

When Amazon first launched, anyone could review anything. Authors' friends flooded the site with five-star ratings. Since then, Amazon has tightened up, reducing the likelihood of phony raves. But the site's book pages continue to be peppered with deceptive reviews, many generated by pay-for-raves websites. It shouldn't be long before artificial intelligence pollutes book reviewing even more.

As mentioned, John Locke used a pay-for-raves site to purchase wholesale deception. In addition, publishers, authors, and their friends have capitalized on the web's anonymity to create alter egos, or "sock puppets," to post puffery masquerading as reviews.

Speaking of "review bombing," in 2013, Michael Jackson fans objected to a book critical of their hero. They bombed it, dropping its Amazon rating from four stars to one. In 2023, the fantasy novelist Cait Corrain admitted review bombing her competition. (Her agent and publisher immediately dropped her.) And authors writing on the Authors Guild community forum have reported blackmail attempts by review bombers who have threatened to pan their books on Amazon and Goodreads unless they pay up. "Books used to die by being ignored," the Cornell University sociologist Trevor Pinch remarked, "but now they can be killed."

Finally, some authors have combined sock puppets and review bombing to do what Ben Franklin did: pummel the competition while lauding their own work. The *New York Times* has estimated that up to one-third of internet book reviews are untrustworthy.

Alas, that may include *Kirkus* reviews. Virginia Kirkus sold her journal in 1962, but it has endured as an esteemed resource for librarians. Neither publishers nor authors pay for *Kirkus* reviews. Libraries subscribe. But as the third book business saw titles skyrocket, *Kirkus* launched a companion review directory, *Kirkus Indie*, which caters to self-publishers and those whose books don't get reviewed by its venerable sibling. *Kirkus Indie* reviews are for sale, costing $425 (seven- to nine-week turnaround) to $575 (four to six weeks). Authors get the last word. They are free to kill pans. If authors allow reviews to go public, they appear not in the *Kirkus Reviews* librarians consult but on KirkusReviews.com, where they may or may not garner any notice. Still, for what it's worth, thumbs-up reviews can be blurbed as coming from *Kirkus*.

As a reader and author, I want honest book reviews. On the other hand, I've sent free copies of my books to friends, asking them to post on Amazon. Many have clicked five stars. I like to think my books have deserved it, but they're friends who got free copies . . .

The upsurge in deceptive reviews devalues *all* book reviews, including those by honorable reviewers. Unfortunately, it's often impossible to distinguish good faith from duplicity.

Book Reviews: Gender Bias

Women read two-thirds of all books, but men write most book reviews. The women's literary organization VIDA tallies book reviewers annually by gender. In 2019, women wrote:

- 33 percent of reviews in the *New York Review of Books*
- 37 percent in the *Atlantic*
- 37 percent in *Harper's Magazine*
- 40 percent in the *Nation*
- 42 percent in the *New Republic*
- 45 percent in the *New Yorker*
- 54 percent in the *New York Times*

Reading at Risk?

Home video players debuted in the 1970s, personal computers in the 1980s, and the internet in the 1990s. They all grabbed eyeballs from other media and triggered anguished (and familiar) predictions of books' imminent demise. The angst spurred the National Endowment for the Arts to survey the reading habits of seventeen thousand Americans. Its 2004 report, *Reading at Risk*, made headlines. It showed that from the 1980s to the millennium, the proportion of adult Americans engaging in recreational reading (not for work or school) declined 10 percent, and among young adults, 17 percent. Pundits bemoaned the looming death of books.

However, other more recent surveys have produced different results:

• A 2005 report by the media investment firm Veronis Suhler Stevenson showed that from 1985 to 2005, Americans spent *increasing* amounts of time reading books.

• A 2016 Pew Research report showed that during the previous year, 73 percent of American adults said they had read at least one book (including e-books and audiobooks).

• Finally, a review of U.S. adult reading from 2011 to 2021 by Statista. com, a compiler of statistics, shows no decline in reading during that decade.

Even *Reading at Risk* hedged its findings: "The proportion of people reading literature is higher than participation in most cultural, sports, and leisure activities. . . . [O]nly TV watching, moviegoing, and exercising attract significantly more people than reading."

Finally, during the COVID pandemic, when Americans largely stayed home surrounded by radio, TV, smartphones, streaming video, social media, and a billion websites, book sales rose. When words ignite the intellect and imagination, the result is so compelling that despite the allure of other media, a substantial proportion of the population still chooses to read books. And an estimated five million Americans regularly forgo other media to discuss them in book groups.

= 21 =

The Meteoric Rise and Decline of E-books

From the Rocket Reader to the Kindle

Since the millennium, e-books have triggered an unprecedented surge in new releases. E-books smoldered for a decade before they caught fire. They debuted quietly in 1998 with the Rocket eBook reader, a $500 device that could hold ten books. Soon after, the SoftBook appeared ($600, 250 books). Both sold poorly. In a 2000 fire sale, the publisher of *TV Guide* bought both devices and melded them into the Gemstar reader. It too flopped, dying quietly in 2003. A few other e-readers came and went, prompting punditry that e-books were an innovation whose time would never arrive. Then in 2007, Amazon launched the Kindle. Similar to its deceased predecessors in size and weight, but cheaper (initially $400), the original Kindle sold out in six hours—and sales of e-books exploded.

The Kindle succeeded for three reasons: trust, convenience, and price. Amazon was already the nation's premiere bookseller. Readers trusted the site and were happy to try its e-reader and e-books. The Kindle was internet-connected. With a few clicks, readers could download up to two hundred titles from Amazon's initial catalogue of ninety thousand e-books—now millions. And Amazon offered e-books for just $9.99, half the price of most trade paperbacks.

The Kindle's success attracted imitators, notably the Nook (2009, originally $259) from Barnes & Noble, which became popular with readers who did not want to patronize Amazon. In 2010, Apple introduced its tablet, the iPad ($500), and adapted iPhones to become e-book readers. Reading on the two devices allowed users to turn e-pages almost anywhere any time. Books can also be read on Android phones.

For eight years, 2007 to 2014, as e-readers proliferated and e-book sales rocketed upward, many commentators predicted a book-business apocalypse. *Print, publishers, and booksellers—all toast!* There was even a (print) book on the subject, *Print Is Dead* (2008). Publishers and booksellers feared their businesses models might collapse.

E-books Read Their Readers

E-books live on the web, which is interactive. Their purveyors not only sell them but also analyze how they're read. Some findings:

Readers are most likely to finish books with short chapters.

The longer the mystery, the more likely readers are to jump to the end to see whodunit.

Less than 10 percent of readers plow all the way through political or economic tomes.

And there's a good reason romance novels, mysteries, and thrillers are called "page-turners." Compared with literary fiction, readers speed through them more quickly. The category read the fastest: erotica.

Fiction Regains Dominance

Recall that during the first book business, fiction dominated. But as the second book business developed, radio dramas, movies, and television met much of readers' needs for stories, and nonfiction surged ahead of fiction. Or so everyone thought.

In the third book business, as e-books (and audiobooks) appeared, fiction unexpectedly soared, particularly self-published genre novels, especially romances. Today, among the millions of e-books self-published annually—more than five thousand a day—the majority are genre fiction. Why? People love good stories, if the price is right.

The third book business has substantially reduced the cost of books. Many e-books sell for a dollar or two. Plenty of readers are happy to take breaks from social media and streaming—and even try authors they've never heard of—if they can buy novels cheap. According to the publishing consultant Mike Shatzkin, "There is a substantial market willing to try storytelling from unknown writers if it is offered at a relatively low price."

What's the Value of an E-book?

In 1998, when the Rocket e-reader launched and e-books were still curiosities, agents and publishers discussed how the new format's income might be divided. E-books required no paper, ink, printing, binding, warehousing, shipping, or disposal of returns—not to mention fewer employees to handle all the eliminated headaches. In *The Art and Science of Book Publishing* (1970), Herbert S. Bailey Jr., the longtime director of Princeton University Press, estimated those costs as a percentage of publishers' total expenses:

Paper, printing, binding	32%
Warehousing and shipping	5%
Returns	14%
TOTAL	51%

E-books cut publishers' costs in half. At least it looked that way initially.

Agents digested those numbers and asserted that authors should receive 50 percent of the gross on e-book sales. Their thinking: The royalty rate for hardcover books was 10 percent; trade paperbacks, 8 percent; mass market, 7 percent. But paperbacks greatly outsold hardbacks. Across print formats, authors' overall royalty rate was around 8.5 percent. If e-book royalties were 50 percent, authors would make an extra 41.5 percent per sale. In a world of plummeting median book sales, that boost would help keep authors writing—and publishers publishing. Meanwhile, publishers would bank an additional 8.5 percent: the 50 percent they saved on e-book production minus the 41.5 percent royalty boost agents advocated. A win-win.

Initially, several publishers agreed to a 50 percent royalty rate on e-books. *Why not? E-books are going nowhere.* But when e-books took off, publishers feared the new format would kill print—and them. Faced with this new existential threat, publishers moved to squeeze every last penny out of e-books. For most contracts, the majors retreated from 50 percent and offered 25 percent. Why that percentage? It's never been explained, but it pacified authors.

Authors thought, *I make 8.5 percent on print but now 25 percent on e-books. How cool is that!* About as cool as getting pickpocketed. Agents and the Authors Guild objected, but reminiscent of the windfall from electronic typesetting, publishers had the leverage to snatch the lion's share of e-book revenue.

While the e-book royalty rate was being debated, three publishers wanted to roll some of my backlist titles into e-books. I'd signed those contracts before anyone imagined e-books, so the publishers asked me to sign riders specifying a royalty rate of 25 percent.

My agent insisted, "Don't sign unless you get 50 percent."

I contacted the publishers. Their response: *You want e-books? Then 25 percent. No signature, no e-books—and not one cent in e-book royalties.*

I signed. What choice did I have?

Today, book contracts are less likely to specify different royalty rates for books' various editions and more likely to offer a single rate based on books' net income, the amount publishers actually receive after granting booksellers discounts. No matter how royalties are calculated, are they honest? Publishers don't open their books, so most authors never know. Only the big names can afford audits. Everyone else must accept publishers' figures on faith.

The Self-Publishing Jackpot: Contracts with the Majors

When a few e-book self-publishers sold huge numbers on Amazon, the majors smelled opportunity. Successful e-books might be rolled into print and sell big. Simon & Schuster offered the e-book spy novelist John Locke and the e-book sci-fi author Hugh Howey lucrative contracts for their print distribution rights. St. Martin's Press picked up the e-book fantasy author Amanda Hocking. And when Amazon sold 350,000 copies of Tracey Garvis Graves's self-published novel (after fourteen rejections from the majors), Plume offered her a rich multibook deal. The majors now use self-published e-books as a farm system, plucking out top sellers to play major league ball.

Some self-publishing advocates have condemned these deals, calling self-publishers who sign with the majors "traitors." But really, they're just people. The major publishers offer not only money but also distribution, publicity, and perhaps greater legitimacy in the eyes of the reading public. Fortune is great, but the combination of fame and fortune is better. It's no surprise that suddenly prominent e-book authors opt for major-publisher contracts.

How many copies must self-publishers sell to attract the majors' attention? Agents estimate one hundred thousand.

The Surprising Decline of E-books

From 2007 to 2013, e-books sales undermined print sales and gave many publishers panic attacks. Then, surprisingly, in 2014, e-book sales topped out and began to fall:

E-book Sales and Revenue (United States)

2014	234 million copies	$1.6 billion
2016	181 million	$1.2 billion
2018	168 million	$1.0 billion
2020	191 million	$1.1 billion˙
2022	160 million	$975 million

˙The pandemic boosted sales.

(Danny McLoughlin, "Ebook Sales Statistics 2023," WordsRated, June 7, 2023, https://wordsrated.com/ebooks-sales-statistics/#:~:text=15.92%20million%20 ebooks%20were%20sold,ebooks%20were%20sold%20per%20hour.)

At their peak in 2014, e-books accounted for 23 percent of trade book sales; in 2022, less than 15 percent. Why the decline? After all, Amazon has sold more than thirty million Kindles, and all tablets and smartphones are e-readers. Yet sales have fallen—for several reasons:

Screen fatigue. At school or work, tens of millions of Americans spend much of their days staring at screens. When they read for pleasure, many would rather not look at screens.

E-books have become genre-specific. Initially, e-books sold significant numbers across all genres. Today, they account for about half of romance fiction sales and a third of mysteries, sci-fi, and fantasy, but less—often a lot less—than 20 percent of most other book categories.

Print books are less likely to get stolen. At the beach, I'd feel fine leaving a book on my blanket, even a hardback. But not an e-reader or tablet.

Print doesn't contribute to insomnia. A 2014 study in the *Proceedings of the National Academy of Sciences* suggests that staring at light-emitting e-books in otherwise dark rooms before retiring may interfere with falling asleep.

Most people prefer print. Many people love physical books—their heft, portability, smell, and touch, including the feel of turning pages. Of course, affection does not guarantee survival, but consider pencils. They were invented around 1560 when English shepherds discovered a large deposit of graphite and used it to mark sheep and subsequently write on paper. Since then, pencils have been joined by fountain pens, ballpoints, markers, you name it. No doubt, pen buffs once predicted the end of pencils, but they're still with us.

Ditto for candles. Experts predicted electric lighting would kill them. Few of us read by candlelight anymore, but for religious rituals, festive occasions, intimate dinners, and sex, Americans' expenditures for candles top $2 billion a year.

And vinyl LPs. During the 1990s, CDs and MP3s virtually wiped them out, but since 2008, vinyl has rebounded, and CDs have faded, replaced by streaming. Go figure.

In 2019, the *New York Times* asked 4,151 subscribers how they preferred to read books. Fewer than three in ten (29 percent) chose e-books. The rest (71 percent) preferred print.

New media rarely replace old. New media *change* their predecessors. In the 1840s, the invention of photography triggered predictions of the demise of painting. At the time, most visual artists made livings painting portraits. But why hire an artist and sit for hours when a photographer could create an equivalent—or superior—image faster for less? However, painting didn't die. It took off in new directions: impressionism, cubism, etc. Today, painting thrives.

When television arrived, pundits predicted the end of radio. Radio *dramas* died as TV grabbed that niche. But radio thrived with music, news, sports, and talk shows. Today it's bigger than ever.

E-books have become just another way to read, along with audiobooks, which now gross $1 billion a year, around the same as e-books.

Likewise, e-books didn't kill print. They changed it. As e-book sales rose, sales of mass-market paperbacks cratered. In 2007, pocket paperbacks accounted for 24 percent of book sales and 15 percent of book revenue. By 2016, those figures had fallen to 10 percent and 6 percent, respectively. Most genre fiction sold as mass-market paperbacks. Those genres have seen major migration to e-books.

Finally, in contrast to what agents and authors had originally thought, e-books did not reduce publishers' costs all that much. Compared with print, e-books cost publishers only half as much per copy, but today e-books account for no more than 15 percent of most publishers' sales, so e-books have decreased publishers' costs only marginally.

=== 22 ===

The Many Challenges of Self-Publishing and the Conundrum of "Quality"

Publishers for Hire—Again

The digital revolution has gifted authors with the ability to self-publish books indistinguishable from the majors' releases. But how?

If authors revel in doing everything themselves, they're free to deal with book design and typesetting, jacket design and cover artists, printers and marketing, sales calls and distribution strategies, not to mention promotion and publicity. But can authors do all that well? Publishing is a complicated profession. Few publishers are also authors, but many authors believe they can also be publishers. Warning: Publishing involves a steep learning curve, a huge time commitment, myriad hassles, and possibly costly mistakes.

For most authors, it's wiser and more cost-efficient to hire a publishing services company (hybrid publisher) that's already set up to produce books. This element of the third book business arrived in 1997, when a Bloomington, Indiana, company launched the first all-digital PSC, Xlibris, from *ex libris*, Latin for "from the library of." Today, Xlibris charges $1,000 to $17,000 for its many publishing packages. The most popular is the $5,000 option. Xlibris copyedits manuscripts and digitally designs, indexes, and prints trade paperbacks and/or hardcovers, with formatting for e-readers. Xlibris also registers copyrights in authors' names and provides Amazon pages and other services. In 2009, Xlibris was acquired by Author Solutions, which owns other PSCs: Author-House, iUniverse, and Booktango. Author Solutions says its imprints have released more than three hundred thousand titles.

In 2000, three years after Xlibris's debut, a PSC called BookSurge launched in South Carolina. In 2005, Amazon acquired it and rechristened it CreateSpace. In 2018, Amazon folded CreateSpace into its e-book operation, Kindle Direct Publishing. KDP charges authors next to nothing to publish, but it offers no editorial services beyond formatting for Kindles and providing Amazon pages for the resulting e-books. Amazon takes 30 percent of sales revenue. KDP releases more than one million titles annually and earns its authors more than $300 million a year. This sounds impressive until you realize that most KDP authors earn less than $300 a year.

Twenty-first-century PSCs also include Blurb, launched in 2005 (14 million titles for 500,000 authors); Smashwords, 2008 (750,000 titles, 200,000 authors); and some five hundred other companies, making hybrid publishing the fastest-growing niche in the book business, the tail that now wags the dog.

Between 1992 and 1997, new ISBNs rose an average of 5 percent per year. But during Xlibris's first year, it attracted authors spurned by agents and publishers, and ISBNs almost doubled. After the millennium, as PSCs proliferated, ISBNs soared:

Year	New books released in the United States
1995	62,039
1998 (the year after Xlibris debuted)	119,262
2007 (as PSCs proliferated)	407,646
2008 (soon after the Kindle appeared)	561,580
2010 to 2022	1.2 to 4.2 million per year (an average of 2.8 million annually)

(Greco, Rodríguez, and Wharton, *The Culture and Commerce of Publishing in the 21st Century, p.* 96, and R.R. Bowker)

Initially, twenty-first-century PSCs gave the major publishers migraines. *They take no risks and profit from every title.* Well, if you can't beat them, join them. In 2012, Penguin, subsequently Penguin Random House, acquired Author Solutions. That same year, Simon & Schuster teamed up with Author Solutions to launch its own in-house PSC imprint, Archway. The majors are not averse to pay-to-play deals as long as authors pay enough. And publisher-owned PSCs give authors legitimacy. Those who publish through Archway can truthfully say, *Simon & Schuster published my book*.

PSCs pose an even greater threat to small presses and medium-size independent publishers. For decades, their bread and butter has been the very authors now tempted by PSCs. As one small-press publisher told me, "In the nineties, we printed five thousand copies and sold three thousand. Today [2015], we print three thousand and hope to sell one thousand, and often don't." Soon after our conversation, that house went bankrupt.

Since the mid-twentieth century, several publishers have avoided bankruptcy by becoming nonprofits, among them: The New Press, Graywolf Press, Milkweed Editions, and Coffee House Press. They solicit tax-deductible grants from wealthy patrons to keep the lights on and cover losses from literary titles that don't earn out. More recently, new nonprofit publishers have joined them, including McSweeney's, founded by the big-name author Dave Eggers. The San Francisco publisher reorganized as a nonprofit in 2014. But nonprofit publishers are very selective, while PSCs are happy to publish anyone willing to write a check.

Going forward, look for publishers of all sizes to embrace the PSC model and go increasingly hybrid, paying production costs for the favored few, while requiring everyone else to pay to publish for around what the Author Solutions companies charge, $5,000 to $20,000.

The hybrid model echoes the late nineteenth-century transition from the first book business to the second. Publishers large and small can easily incorporate the PSC model into their operations. They're set up to release books. As typical sales of new releases have declined, the PSC model throws a lifeline. Authors pay to publish, and like colonial printers, PSCs profit from every title, even if those books never find audiences.

Some authors cringe at paying to publish. But as the third book business matures, I expect most to realize that the hybrid model is a product of twenty-first-century publishing necessity.

Listen closely, and you can hear the culture changing. Publishers no longer denigrate self-publishing as the last refuge of losers who can't attract real publishers. These days they're more likely to say, *If authors won't invest in their own books, why should we?*

I'm acquainted with a young assistant professor who, in 2013, confronted the academic imperative to either publish or perish. No academic press would shoulder the cost of turning her dissertation into a book. But one liked her manuscript and had a PSC arm. She invested $6,000 and added a book to her CV. Wise move. That book helped her land a tenure-track job.

Gatekeeping and "Taste": The Conundrum of "Quality"

As the second book business developed, new releases soared and publishers railed about too many books, most of which were pulp paperbacks they considered "trash." The third book business has resurrected the notion of too many books, but instead of dismissing e-books as trash, publishers and bibliophiles have opted for a more nuanced spin on the same dismissal, asserting that in a world without gatekeepers, literary quality has suffered. Really?

How books get published has nothing to do with their quality. Self-publishing was the bedrock of the first book business. Emerson, Thoreau, Longfellow, Whitman, Frederick Douglass, and Harriet Beecher Stowe are just a few of the many noted nineteenth-century authors who self-published or published with the help of wealthy patrons. In the second book business, the threat of bestselling authors self-publishing threatened the new publisher-centric model and gave twentieth-century publishers insomnia, among them literary legend André Schiffrin (1935–2013), who for thirty years was head of Pantheon. From his 2000 memoir: "The fear that best-selling authors might publish their own work has haunted the conglomerates for many years now. . . . They know that the Stephen Kings of this world can easily hire printers and distributors."

Publishers held on to top authors by offering huge advances, outsized royalty rates, and multibook deals. But they rightly feared that the siren song of self-publishing might still seduce the biggest names. So publishers invoked the same snobbery that kept pulp fiction out of bookshops. They stigmatized self-publishing. The publishers' PR campaign hit a grand slam. For centuries, self-publishing had been the dominant model, the *only* model. But by the 1930s, it was toxic and remained so for seventy years.

Which raises a question. What distinguishes greatness from garbage? If there were clear criteria, one would expect publishers to embrace the former and shun the latter. But one glance at publishers' track record raises serious questions about their ability to distinguish quality from trash. Here are some of the many titles major publishers rejected before someone deigned to release them:

- *Harry Potter*, J.K. Rowling, nine rejections before acceptance
- *The Naked and the Dead*, Norman Mailer, twelve rejections
- *A Time to Kill*, John Grisham, twelve
- *The Diary of Anne Frank*, sixteen
- *M*A*S*H*, Richard Hooker, seventeen
- *Lord of the Flies*, William Golding, twenty
- *Dubliners*, James Joyce, twenty-two
- *Catch-22*, Joseph Heller, twenty-two
- *Dune*, Frank Herbert, twenty-three
- *A Wrinkle in Time*, Madeleine L'Engle, twenty-six
- *Carrie*, Stephen King, thirty
- *Gone with the Wind*, Margaret Mitchell, thirty-eight
- *Zen and the Art of Motorcycle Maintenance*, Robert Pirsig, 121
- This book. I stopped counting at twenty

Who anointed publishing people gatekeepers, anyway? So, they're in the book business—so what? They're just like the rest of us, people with opinions. Their decisions usually have less to do with "quality" than with their assessment of books' commercial appeal—which they have some difficulty discerning.

One myopic gatekeeper was the big-name novelist William Styron, who portrayed his experiences as those of the character Stingo in the opening pages of *Sophie's Choice*. World War II had just ended, and he was fresh out of college, a wide-eyed southern boy in the Big Apple. Agents didn't become de rigeur for another decade. Publishers hired Styron and other young English majors to read the slush pile.

Styron perused one manuscript by a nutty Norwegian who'd built a raft in Peru and sailed to Polynesia to prove his silly theory that ancient South Americans might have colonized the South Pacific. *Sorry, Mr. Heyerdahl, your manuscript does not meet our current needs.*

Styron wasn't alone. Nineteen other houses rejected that manuscript. So imagine Styron's surprise when, in 1948, *The Kon-Tiki Expedition* became a bestselling international sensation whose movie adaptation won an Academy Award in 1952.

Editors and publishers insist they value artistry and profundity. But scan the majors' catalogues. How much of either do you see? Many releases are as ephemeral as the crossword puzzles that launched Simon & Schuster. While publishers have never released books "at random," they've always gone with their guts . . . leavened by fads, personal connections, and the desire to lock up noted authors.

Today, with e-books, publishers' ability to spot quality continues to be questionable. A 2012 study tracked the Amazon ratings of seven thousand genre e-books. Those published by the majors averaged 4.1 out of 5, and self-published titles, 4.4. Readers *preferred* the self-published titles. English professors might insist that quality writing is distinct from trash, but beyond embracing *The Elements of Style* and *The Chicago Manual of Style*, how do we recognize it?

By worshipping the classics? Until recently, canonical authors have virtually all been white men.

Popularity? Recall the early condemnations of bestseller lists and bibliophiles' insistence that sales have nothing to do with quality. In addition, the popularity effect shows that many bestsellers are more lucky than great.

Awards? They simply reflect the judges' opinions. I've judged journalism contests. The process was less about quality than who argued loudest for personal favorites.

Reviews? Book reviewing began as a dirty business. Has it become cleaner? I know an author who coveted a blurb from a big name. She reviewed the man's latest book and—surprise!—loved it. After her puff piece appeared, she got her quote.

Quality is subjective. Several big names have published under pseudonyms. In the 1980s, reviews of two books by Jane Somers ranged from chilly to frigid. But when Somers was revealed to be the Nobel Prize–winning novelist Doris Lessing (1919–2013), suddenly the critics lavished praise. In 2013, tepid reviews greeted *The Cuckoo's Calling*, a detective novel by Robert Galbraith. But when the world learned that Galbraith was J. K. Rowling of Harry Potter fame, suddenly *Cuckoo* was terrific.

Is any writer universally venerated as a great? Yes, William Shakespeare (1564-1616). Four hundred years after his death, the Bard's plays are fixtures of high school and college curricula. They're produced more frequently than plays by any other playwright living or dead. Shakespeare festivals pepper the landscape. His hometown is a tourist attraction, and his Globe Theater has been resurrected. More than any other writer in English, Shakespeare is revered.

But after his death, Shakespeare was almost forgotten until publication of his collected plays in the *First Folio* (1623). Subsequently, he was respected, but remained controversial. Ministers groaned about his violence, and moralists excoriated his raunchiness. During the late nineteenth century, all was forgiven as Shakespeare became venerated. Noting the evolution of opinion, George Bernard Shaw (1856-1950) dubbed it "bardolotry."

Is Shakespeare quality? Today, unquestionably, but over the centuries, many eminent critics have thought otherwise. Which is why I insist that literary quality has always been a matter of fickle opinion.

Those opinions sometimes prove fatal. A novel by John Kennedy Toole (1937-1969) was rejected so many times that he descended into depression, and at age thirty-one committed suicide. His mother pursued his manuscript's publication. Ten years and dozens more rejections later, she showed it to noted Southern novelist Walker Percy (1916-1990). He loved it and persuaded his publisher to release it. In 1981, *A Confederacy of Dunces* became a bestseller and won the Pulitzer Prize.

Debate about the pros and cons of gatekeeping dominated publishing during the first decade of this century. Then the controversy faded as major publishers launched PSCs and book people became accustomed to a world awash in millions of new self-published releases every year.

The Two Main Problems with Self-Publishing: Little if Any Editing and Shoddy Manufacture

From 1949 to 2012, one PSC, Vantage Press, littered magazines with classified ads proclaiming, "Publish Your Book." Publishers derided Vantage as a vanity press. I read one Vantage release, a novel set in a Caribbean scuba resort about the life and loves of a dive master. In my opinion, it was the literary equivalent of fingernails on a blackboard. But many publishers' releases are equally awful. The issue is not who publishes books but how they're written—and edited.

That scuba novel actually had potential. The characters were *almost* interesting, the plot *almost* engaging. With developmental guidance, line editing, and copyediting, it might have been worth recommending to friends. But it read like it had been dashed off in a weekend by an author who never cracked a thesaurus. The real problem with self-publishing is that authors often rush their work into print. These days, rushing into print is easier than ever, thanks to Sqribble, a PSC website authors can use to publish e-books almost instantly for less than $100.

In *On Writing: A Memoir of the Craft*, Stephen King notes: "To write is human, to edit is divine." Attention, self-publishers: Before you release your work, get it edited. Extensively. The great downfall of self-publishing is insufficient editing. If there's one truth I've learned from four decades as an author and ten years as a magazine editor, it's that *every* writer needs editors. Authors can revise manuscripts until they can't see straight, but they *cannot* edit themselves. As writers gain experience, some believe they outgrow editing. *Au contraire.* Excellent writers need excellent editors who can discern minor deficiencies. It doesn't matter if you're an aspiring author or a big name, every manuscript needs more than one pair of eyes—and in my opinion, the more the better. A good fifty people—family, friends, and several professional editors—critiqued the various drafts of this book.

When self-published titles are well edited, they can be great reads. Two come to mind, both rejected by legions of publishers. One was a political vampire novel, the other a memoir of addiction recovery. In my opinion, the former was very good, the latter, outstanding—in large part because several editors had pushed the authors to do their best work.

The other problem with self-publishing is poorly manufactured books. That Vantage scuba novel fell apart by the time I finished it. These days, print-on-demand companies can produce books indistinguishable from the majors, but caveat emptor. Before you print, say, five hundred copies, pay a little extra to have a proof copy printed so you can check the cover, binding, paper, and print quality.

National Warehousing but Not Distribution

With self-published e-books and print-on-demand, publishers lost their monopoly on book manufacturing. Why should authors still publish with them? One key reason is national distribution. The majors—and smaller publishers who distribute through them—have sophisticated distribution systems that move books reasonably efficiently from printers to warehouses to bookstores, a benefit the hybrid houses and self-publishing platforms can't match.

Distribution has always bedeviled publishers. Today, it's just as daunting and more important than ever. With book shelf life down to a few months or less, new releases have scant chance of selling unless they're displayed front and center when publicity and reviews (if any) appear.

Digital book production threatens publisher-centrism, but the majors' virtual lock on distribution keeps their titles in booksellers' front windows. Until the millennium, the two major distributors, Ingram of LaVergne, Tennessee, and Baker & Taylor of Charlotte, North Carolina, worked hand in glove with the majors and well-established indie publishers, but not with self-publishers. (B&T has since left trade distribution to focus on school and public libraries.)

Ingram's near monopoly on trade distribution has earned the company a powerful perch. But instead of celebrating, the nation's top book distributor got nervous. When e-books took off, Ingram realized that electronic publishing threatened its survival—fewer print books to distribute, so less income. In response, Ingram reinvented itself as a "content distributor."

In 1996, Ingram established an in-house print-on-demand company, Lightning Source, geared toward self-publishing authors. Printing with Lightning offered a unique perk: inclusion in Ingram's vast book database. This meant instant national bookstore availability to any author who printed with Lightning. (More recently, Ingram has established a similar subsidiary, IngramSpark, which provides near-instant print-on-demand of small runs for publishers.)

Say book buyers want your Lightning-printed title, but their local bookstores don't stock it. Any bookseller can find it in Ingram's database. Lightning prints, Ingram ships, and a few days later, the bookstore invites the buyer to pick up the book. Unfortunately, there's a big difference between including books in Ingram's vast database and placing them on bookstore shelves. Ingram may be the nation's book distributor, but its print-on-demand operation does not provide national distribution, just electronic *warehousing*.

Of course, inclusion in Ingram's database is preferable to exclusion. It moves titles one step closer to buyers. However, that's usually so near yet so far. How many buyers ask for books not on the shelves? Some, but not many. Book purchases are often impulse buys. If buyers don't see what they want, the impulse quickly passes. So, despite easy availability through Ingram, the typical self-published title printed by Lightning garners no more attention than a blade of grass on a golf course.

Twenty-First-Century Piracy: Digital Spurs Theft

As we have seen, the book business was founded on piracy, and the digital revolution has made it easier and more rapacious than ever. Today, with scanners and digital printing, anyone can churn out counterfeit books and sell them on Amazon alongside the real thing. Amazon insists it moves heaven and earth to take down pirated titles. The site says it has terminated the accounts of more than one million booksellers suspected of hawking them. The Authors Guild helps authors demand take-downs. The Guild has also chided Amazon for doing little to keep counterfeit books off its site in the first place.

Meanwhile, dozens of other websites scoff at copyright by selling pirated e-books. Former Authors Guild president Scott Turow searched "Scott Turow free e-books" and discovered many sites offering pirate editions of his novels. Search other big names and you find the same thing: pirate sites offering huge catalogues of stolen books for free once you pay the modest subscription fee.

Media counterfeiting has become a huge problem. Authors, filmmakers, and other copyright holders send fifty million take-down demands annually. But it's Whac-A-Mole. What gets taken down goes right back up elsewhere. "Modern infringement," says the Marquette University law professor Bruce Boyden, "is persistent, ubiquitous, and gargantuan in scale. . . . Takedown notices, with their detailed requirements and elaborate back-and-forth, are a poor way to achieve the routine policing of sites that receive thousands of new files every hour."

Like shoplifters, buyers of pirated e-books tend to be young people. My nonfiction deals with health—not a big draw for most adolescents and young adults—so the pirates have shown little interest. But in 2014, an indie press published my cannabis murder mystery, *Killer Weed*, which follows three San Francisco marijuana merchants through forty years of pot dealing. Shortly after its release, *Killer Weed* was pirated.

Book pirates operate in a shadowy realm, but the stolen property they sell appears on web pages that carry advertising. Consequently, search engines profit from the sale of stolen goods. Should they be held accountable?

The search engines don't think so. *We're no more responsible for pirates using our sites than the federal government is for thieves shipping stolen property through the mail.*

That's a false analogy. The search engines mint money by placing paid ads next to book pirates' listings. Scott Turow: "If I stood on a corner telling people who asked where they could buy stolen goods and collected a small fee for it, I'd be on my way to jail. And yet even while search engines sail under mottos like 'Don't be evil,' they do the same thing."

Particularly Google. Until 2011, the company placed ads beside its pirate-site search results and coined money while authors and publishers got ripped off. After lawsuits, Google pulled those ads. But the company still profits from book theft. Google queries for pirated books draw eyeballs to its search results, and once there, many visitors click to other pages containing paid advertising.

Google is also a leader in another form of twenty-first-century piracy, abuse of "fair use," the idea that small portions of copyrighted material can be legally quoted in reviews, news stories, scholarly works, and parody. In 2004, Google partnered with several libraries to digitize millions of books still protected by copyright, without authors' or publishers' permission and without paying anything to copyright holders.

The Authors Guild and the Association of American Publishers sued, claiming infringement. Google and the libraries countered that digitization showed only snippets—in their view, fair use.

In 2015, a U.S. court of appeals ruled in favor of Google and the libraries. The Supreme Court declined to review the decision. The appeals court called digitization fair use that "benefits all society" while "respecting authors' rights." Funny, this author feels the opposite of respected.

However, in 2023, authors and publishers gained a victory against fair-use abuse when a federal judge ordered the Internet Archive to stop its wholesale unlicensed copying of entire books. (For information on removing books from the Internet Archive, contact the Authors Guild.)

As this book goes to press, digitizing whole books and releasing some of their content is fine, but releasing entire books is not. That leaves a key question unanswered: What proportion of digitized books can pirates—I mean *archivists*—release without paying creators and publishers? The courts have yet to decide.

Copyright and patents are enshrined in the Constitution, making authors and inventors the only two occupations expressly granted constitutional protection. But today, digital book piracy has become so easy, so rampant, and often so legal that one wonders if copyright retains any meaning at all.

=== 23 ===

Backlist Gold and Mass-Market Hardcovers, as the Biggest Names Become Their Own Co-Publishers

The Biggest Merger: Penguin Random House

In 1980, there were two dozen major publishers. Then the third book business upended the industry. Self-publishing squeezed publishers' incomes and market shares, forcing many into bankruptcy—or mergers that turned them into imprints, ghosts of those former houses. By 2012, only a half dozen majors remained, the Big Six.

In 2013, Penguin and Random House, the two largest of the Big Six, merged into Penguin Random House (PRH), creating a mega-publisher that dwarfed the competition. PRH accounted for 40 percent of major publisher trade book revenue. Publishing consultant Mike Shatzkin quipped that the PRH merger turned the Big Six not into the Big Five, but into the Big One and Trailing Four:

1. Penguin Random House, a division of the German media conglomerate Bertelsmann, owns Anchor, Ballantine, Bantam, Berkley, Broadway, Delacorte, Dell, Doubleday, Dutton, G. P. Putnam's Sons, Golden Books, Tarcher Books (now TarcherPerigee), Jove, Knopf, New American

Library, Pantheon, Plume, Signet, Schocken, Viking, Vintage, and more than two hundred other imprints. Sales in 2021: $4.7 billion.

2. Hachette (a French publisher) owns Fawcett, Warner, Grand Central Publishing, and Little, Brown, among others. Sales in 2022: $3 billion.

3. HarperCollins is owned by Rupert Murdoch's News Corporation, originally Australian, now headquartered in New York. It owns Harper, Avon, William Morrow, and other imprints. Sales in 2022: $2.2 billion.

4. Simon & Schuster is owned by the private equity firm Kohlberg Kravis Roberts & Company (American). S&S owns Scribner, Fireside, Touchstone, and Pocket Books, among others. Sales in 2022: $1 billion.

5. Macmillan, owned by Holtzbrinck (German), owns Times Books, Henry Holt, St. Martin's, Farrar, Straus & Giroux, and other imprints. Sales in 2021: $1 billion.

The PRH merger was unusual. This wasn't your typical brink-of-bankruptcy desperation sale. Neither house was in financial jeopardy. Why did they merge?

Financial analysts cited two reasons: efficiency and Amazon. By combining, PRH could eliminate "redundancies"—that is, employees—forcing survivors to work harder to manage the combined company's larger list. And PRH's size and clout might help in contract negotiations with the big bully, Amazon.

But the analysts missed the real reason. By combining, PRH boasted a much larger backlist—just as old titles gained unprecedented value.

New gold from old titles? Chris Anderson, editor of *Wired*, explained it in his 2006 book, *The Long Tail: Why the Future of Business Is Selling Less of More*. The book offered a fresh take on information products, notably movies. Anderson analyzed DVD rentals by Netflix (before the company pivoted to streaming). Most customers rented recent blockbusters, the "big head." But many also rented everything else, "the long tail." Every year, Netflix notched at least one rental of 98 percent of the movies in its huge catalogue. Netflix coined money renting big-head movies to a huge audience. But it also scored considerable income renting its vast inventory of long-tail films a few times every year—or, as Anderson put it, selling less of more.

Publishers also had a long tail, their backlists. Recall that fledgling Random House paid its bills from sales of its large Modern Library backlist. During the blockbuster era, bankers refused to accept publishers' backlists as collateral for loans. The bankers didn't understand publishing. Big backlists had always been golden. The third book business has turned them into platinum—by offering publishers a lucrative way to cash in on sudden, unanticipated demand.

As the major publishers lost market share to an avalanche of self-published books, what could they do to stanch the hemorrhaging? They could release more new titles. But that meant boosting overhead—more editors, printing, etc.—when today only 6 percent of front list releases sell more than a thousand copies. A bad bet. However, the combination of impulse buying and the long tail allowed publishers to mine gold from their backlists.

In pre-digital, pre-Amazon 1990, if headlines spotlighted any subject— quilting, dinosaurs, Agatha Christie, Eleanor Roosevelt, whatever—and publishers had backlist titles dealing with the fascination du jour, what happened? Assuming that booksellers stocked those titles, they sold. But in the best case, most booksellers stocked only a few copies. Meanwhile, by the time copies could be shipped from warehouses or printed, the impulse to buy had usually evaporated. This left publishers woefully unable to fully capitalize on brief surges of sudden interest.

But in the third book business, all backlist titles sport spiffy Amazon pages. If book buyers suddenly crave books in any niche and publishers have backlist titles, Amazon efficiently captures *all* those impulse orders. Publishers print pre-sold books and surf successive waves of sudden interest all the way to the bank.

After Penguin and Random House merged, their backlist was by far the largest. Even if some PRH releases by big names flopped and competition from e-books reduced sales of the rest of the house's front list, thanks to Amazon and ultra-fast digital printing, their long tail could keep them in business.

Impulse Buying Contributes to *Half* of Book Sales

In 2007, R. R. Bowker, the company that issues ISBNs, surveyed American book buyers about their purchasing decisions at bookstores. Just 43 percent said their buys were completely planned—that is, they visited booksellers to buy specific titles and bought them. More than half of purchases, 57 percent, involved some degree of impulse. Either buyers wandered into bookstores not intending to buy anything but made purchases, or they intended to buy but not what they actually bought.

Print Thrives with "Mass-Market Hardcovers"

Until the 1980s, bookstores rarely carried more than twenty thousand titles. Then Bookstop, a Texas chain, opened superstores offering one hundred thousand. In 1989, Barnes & Noble acquired Bookstop and rolled out superstores nationally. Borders and a few independents followed, including Powell's in Portland, Oregon, and Tattered Cover in Denver. Book buyers loved the selection. By 2006, B&N had 695 superstores, and Borders, 500. Superstores boosted fixed costs: higher rent for all the floor space, more staff and payroll, more inventory, and more returns shipped at the superstores' expense. Profit depended on selling more books faster than ever.

That's exactly what happened. In 1970, typical bestsellers sold one hundred thousand hardcover copies. A decade later, blockbusters sold five hundred thousand. In 2009, one Harry Potter book sold one million hardcover copies the day it appeared. Soon after, Dan Brown's *The Da Vinci Code* (2003) sold a record-shattering eighty million copies. And in 2011, *Fifty Shades of Grey* dwarfed them all. By 2019, after just nine years in print, it had sold 150 million copies, making it number three on the all-time list of the top-selling novels, after *Don Quixote* (published in two parts in 1605 and 1615, an estimated five hundred million copies sold) and *A Tale of Two Cities* (1859, 200 million).

Meanwhile, Walmart et al. began offering blockbusters at discounts that undercut the superstores. Amazon also super-discounted bestsellers. This produced a phenomenon no publisher ever imagined, the "mass-market hardback."

Recall that publishers and booksellers feared that paperbacks, both trade and mass market, might kill hardcover books. But unexpectedly, after the millennium, hardcovers thrived. One reason was price. In 1980, most hardbacks cost $25. Today they usually cost somewhat more, $27 to $30. But during the past forty years, the Consumer Price Index has approximately doubled. In 1980 dollars, today's hardbacks cost only around $15.

The other reason was discounting. Amazon, the superstores, and Walmart sold $25 hardcovers for well under $20, close to the price of trade paperbacks. Books are popular gifts. Many gift-givers thought, *For another buck, I can give a hardback.* Hardcover books went mass market and thrived. They now account for around one-quarter of book sales, with trade paperbacks about 50 percent; e-books, 14 percent; audio-books, 10 percent; and mass-market paperbacks down to just 3 percent.

By 2005, Amazon's eleventh anniversary, it accounted for 40 percent of book sales, with independent booksellers' share around 20 percent. Meanwhile, Walmart and Amazon sucked sales from the superstores that needed a steady supply of blockbusters to make their nut. But how often does a *Da Vinci Code* come along? Not often enough for Borders, which went bankrupt in 2011.

Publishers Fret about Amazon

It didn't take long for publishers to have doubts about Amazon. The site sold mountains of books and returned very few, making it most publishers' most profitable account. But Amazon demanded larger wholesale discounts than publishers typically granted and, after a while, insisted on substantial "promotional fees," a possible synonym for "kickbacks."

Publishers also felt ambivalent as Amazon drove Borders and three-quarters of independent booksellers out of business. But in the end, publishers didn't care who sold books as long as someone did—and no one sold them like Amazon.

Then came the Kindle. Recall that Amazon initially priced e-books at $9.99 and happily took a loss on every sale to move more $400 readers. When the Kindle took off, Amazon instantly controlled 90 percent of the e-book market.

Publishers figured that e-book prices would eventually rise, but Amazon held fast to $9.99—and demanded its huge discount off that price, leaving only crumbs for publishers, who feared that Amazon's demands might bankrupt them. Publishers also chafed at the site's rising promotional fees, initially 3 to 5 percent of publishers' gross on the site, today reportedly 5 to 7 percent.

One publisher declined to fork over the promotional fee, and the "Buy Now" buttons disappeared from its titles' Amazon pages. When the publisher paid, the buttons reappeared. As that tale made the rounds, publishers decided the indies were right. "The Evil Empire" threatened their survival.

In 2010, when Apple released the iPad and its iTunes Store began selling e-books, Apple knew that publishers resented the huge discounts Amazon demanded. Apple dumped discounting and offered publishers an "agency model." Apple invited publishers to set their own e-book prices, with Apple, as sales agent, taking 30 percent.

The majors loved regaining price control, but what should they charge? It had to be more than Amazon's $9.99 but less than what trade paperbacks cost. The publishers batted it around and eventually settled on $12.95. Soon after, Amazon's e-book market share dropped to 60 percent.

The following year, 2011, Amazon launched an in-house publishing operation, stunning the majors. Amazon was no longer just a rapacious bookseller. Now it was *competition*.

The majors feared Amazon Publishing might offer big names advances they couldn't match. Or guarantee home-page placement and saturation marketing. Or cut prices and undersell everyone else. Or refuse to sell other publishers' titles. If any of those nightmares came true, the majors were dead and buried. Clearly, the Evil Empire was a predatory monopoly that had to be stopped. But how?

The major publishers contacted the Justice Department, accusing Amazon of price-fixing and illegally monopolizing e-books. The Justice

Department investigated and acted quickly, filing accusations of price-fixing not against Amazon, but against *Apple and the majors*.

The government considered its case open-and-shut. Amazon sold e-books for $9.99. Apple and the publishers had clearly conspired to raise prices to $12.95, which harmed consumers—classic price-fixing.

Publishers were flabbergasted. *Wait! We're the good guys. It's Amazon that's evil.*

The DoJ: *Amazon's price is lower than yours. Amazon is not hurting consumers. You are.*

Publishers: *But Amazon is killing us!*

The DoJ: *Nonsense. You gross billions.*

Publishers: *What if Amazon boycotts our titles?*

The DoJ: *Tough. No federal law compels anyone to sell anything.*

Publishers: *But we're venerable! Amazon can't just steal our industry.*

The DoJ: *Why not? New business models replace old ones daily. If Amazon's is better than yours, too bad.*

The case generated headlines and hand-wringing. Eventually, the majors and Apple agreed to stop price-fixing. Subsequently, for reasons that remain obscure, Amazon switched to Apple's 30 percent agency model. Publishers, including self-publishers, set prices for their e-books and earn 70 percent. However, Amazon reserves the right to discount prices and extract promotional fees. (Note to self-publishers: Set your price, but don't be surprised if Amazon changes it.)

If the majors believed that $9.99 was "too low" for e-books, they better fasten their seat belts. Today, plenty of e-books are offered for prices ranging from $1 to $5. Mark Coker, CEO of Smashwords, says the price that moves the most e-books on his site is three cents per one thousand words—for a typical sixty-thousand-word title, $1.80.

The Rejuvenation of Back-of-the-Room Sales

Ever since colonial authors sold their books after lectures, back-of-the-room sales have remained a fixture of bookselling and a reliable source of meager to modest income for many authors. During the late twentieth-century heyday of bookstores, booksellers hosted author readings and rang up back-of-the-room sales. But as Amazon drove most booksellers out of business, sales at bookstore author events faded. Fortunately, another sales opportunity appeared: book festivals.

Contemporary book festivals debuted in 1976 in Colorado with Aspen Summer Words. Since the millennium, they have proliferated to more than eighty. A partial list:

- National Book Festival, Washington, D.C. (launched in 2001)
- Litquake, San Francisco (2002)
- Saints and Sinners LGBTQ+ Literary Festival, New Orleans (2003)
- PEN World Voices Festival, New York (2004)
- Portland Book Festival (formerly Wordstock), Oregon (2005)
- Alabama Book Festival (2006)
- Brooklyn Book Festival, New York (2006)
- Hollywood Book Festival, California (2006)
- Pebble Beach (formerly Carmel) Authors and Ideas Festival, California (2007)
- Savannah Book Festival, Georgia (2008)
- Boston Book Festival (2009)
- Tucson Festival of Books, Arizona (2009)
- Bay Area Book Festival, San Francisco (2015)

Festivals spotlight big names to draw crowds but include many other authors, often locals, and everyone sells books at the back of the room or at festival bookstores. Festivals provide authors with two rare and valuable benefits: direct contact with a broad cross section of readers, and seeing their books actually sell.

Note: Some businesses offer to "represent" books at festivals—if authors pay a fee. The Authors Guild calls this a scam and advises authors not to fall for it.

Editors Squeezed, Authors Hurt

In 1980, *Publishers Weekly* surveyed the salaries of major publishers' editorial employees. Top executives made big bucks, but entry-level pay was "absurd and getting worse. . . . Only college graduates with rich parents willing to subsidize them can afford to work in editorial jobs anymore."

Fast-forward to 2023. After a three-month strike, employees of HarperCollins ratified a contract that raised the house's annual base pay to $47,500—a pittance in New York City.

The combination of low pay, mergers that cut staff, relentless pressure to produce bestsellers, and the hypercompetitiveness of the third book business explains why editors now come and go faster than a game of musical chairs. And rapid turnover explains why publishers sometimes write off titles before their release, another lesson I learned the hard way.

These days, authors are lucky if a single editor shepherds their books from signing to publication. Lucky because that editor has a career investment in the books they sign and a reason to tout them to the publisher and sales force. Publishing people sincerely hope every title sells, but in practice, editors who inherit titles left by departed predecessors usually feel less inclined to champion them. Hand-me-downs don't generate the same feeling of ownership, and adoption of "orphan" titles is less likely to advance careers.

Several of my books have had two editors. The second editors initially professed enthusiasm but often dropped the ball. Not that they kissed me off entirely. But they were hardly my advocates.

My worst editorial experience involved a 2009 book about osteoporosis. It had three editors: The first offered the contract but left shortly after I signed. The second departed as I emailed the finished manuscript. The third inherited my orphan, and despite my agent's best efforts and my own charm-offensive trip to New York to woo her, she consigned it to the back burner, then turned off the gas. The first and second editors had assured us that the house would print bound galleys to attract blurbs and reviews. The third never ordered them. My agent protested and I scrambled, emailing PDFs everywhere. I landed some blurbs, but at that time, *Library Journal*, *Booklist*, and *Kirkus* insisted on print copies and wouldn't review my PDF, which torpedoed sales. Most public libraries don't acquire titles unless they've been respectably reviewed in the trades. I paid my publicist extra to hound the trades, but no luck.

I could name the publisher, a venerable major. Other publishers would probably say, *That would* never *happen at* our *house.* I beg to differ. With a third editor arriving at the last minute, the same thing might happen anywhere. The more editors, the less chance of success—and these days, as editors get dizzy spinning in publishing's revolving door, authors who don't pen bestsellers suffer the consequences.

With no trade reviews, that book, *Building Bone Vitality*, coauthored by the University of North Carolina professor Amy Lanou, PhD, was in danger of stillbirth. I went into promotional overdrive and got lucky. The

New York Times personal health columnist became intrigued and wrote a lovely piece that attracted attention. So, despite editor number three's best efforts to kill that title, it earned out, sold well for several years, and continues to sell as part of the long tail.

The Biggest Names Have Become Their Own Co-Publishers

Why do big-name authors still have publishers? The handful of literary stars haven't needed them for years. What sells their books isn't the publisher's name but *theirs*.

The late Jason Epstein: "Name-brand authors need publishers only to print and advertise their books and distribute them to the chains and other mass outlets, routine tasks that all publishers manage equally well and which can be performed as efficiently by independent contractors [PSCs] available for hire. . . . In effect, name-brand authors are already their own publishers, while their nominal publishers are a vestigial, non-essential convenience, beneficiaries (or victims) of inertia on the part of agents reluctant to forgo the security of a publisher's guarantee. When the conglomerates tire, as they eventually must, of overpaying these star performers, their agents may choose either to produce their clients' books themselves or risk losing their golden eggs to business managers who will do the job for them."

One of the nation's biggest-name authors is James Patterson. In 2014 alone, his books sold twenty million copies. His total sales top three hundred million in a dozen languages. For a 2014 profile, Patterson's publisher told the *New York Times* that he's "at the very least co-publisher of his own books." The *Times* called the arrangement "unconventional."

Hardly. I bet that if every big name came clean, we'd find that they too have become co-publishers of their work. They could self-publish, but why bother? Printing, distribution, and marketing are hassles that publishers are happy to manage. So top authors partner with them. The houses earn some money and bragging rights about publishing big names, but the stars make most of the money.

In 2013, Patterson signed a multibook deal worth a reported $150 million. For its duration, he remains a co-publisher. But when his contract expires, who knows what he might do next?

=== 24 ===

Everyone Struggles with Amazon

Revenge of the Indies

By 2015, Amazon had driven most independent booksellers out of business and reduced survivors' market share to around 20 percent. But ironically, in one regard, brick-and-mortar Davids knocked Goliath to the canvas—by boycotting Amazon Publishing.

In 2011, when Amazon Publishing launched, publishers feared it might bury them. Their anxiety grew when Amazon hired a top literary agent, Larry Kirshbaum, to head its new publishing division. He signed several big-name authors for major bucks. Given Amazon's visibility and marketing muscle, book people assumed Amazon's titles would soar. Then independent booksellers and Barnes & Noble announced their boycott. Amazon scoffed. To survive, booksellers must sell books, especially bestsellers. If Amazon published them, how could booksellers refuse those sales?

But the indies stuck to their guns, and the boycott proved surprisingly effective. Sales of Amazon Publishing's initial releases were disappointing. Its big names fled, and its high-profile head resigned. Subsequently, Amazon Publishing combined with the site's Kindle Direct operation and morphed into a PSC, finding great success publishing genre fiction, much of which now sells as e-books. Amazon's imprints include: Montlake (romance), Thomas & Mercer (mysteries and thrillers), and 47North (fantasy, horror, and science fiction).

In 2013, Amazon published only 4 percent of genre titles, but thanks to its juggernaut promotional machine, it earned 15 percent of genre book revenue. Amazon has positioned itself as the "e-pulp" purveyor of the future. Until the millennium, the major publishers had dozens of genre imprints that sold millions of copies annually. Now increasingly those sales have migrated to Amazon, with two results: publishing is becoming more sales-centric, and the majors are losing sleep as their market share continues to shrink.

Amazon Battles Hachette and Authors Take Sides

Amazon and publishers divide book revenue based on multiyear contracts. In 2014, Amazon's agreement with Hachette, the second largest of the Big Five, expired and negotiations hit an impasse. The details were never disclosed, but it took no crystal ball to see that Amazon wanted a larger share of Hachette sales revenue. Whatever Amazon demanded, Hachette refused—and the website got tough:

• Amazon is noted for rapid delivery, but suddenly it took weeks to obtain Hachette titles.

• Amazon discounts prices, but discounts vanished from Hachette books, making them more expensive and less attractive.

• Amazon pioneered preordering of forthcoming titles, but the "Pre-order" buttons for Hachette releases disappeared.

• Finally, on Hachette books' pages, Amazon urged consumers to buy similar titles at lower cost from *other publishers.*

One Hachette release caught in the conflict was *The Everything Store: Jeff Bezos and the Age of Amazon*, by Brad Stone, who remarked, "A book detailing Amazon's heavy-handed tactics in business negotiations becomes . . . a victim of those tactics."

Incensed authors formed an organization, Authors United, which spent $100,000 to publish a full-page petition in the *New York Times* objecting to Amazon's tactics. More than nine hundred authors signed, including many big names. An excerpt: "As writers—most of us not published by Hachette—we feel strongly that no bookseller should block the sale of books. . . . Without taking sides on the contractual dispute between Hachette and Amazon, we encourage Amazon in the strongest possible terms to stop harming the livelihood of the authors on whom it has built its business. None of us, neither readers nor authors, benefit when books are taken hostage."

But many authors who self-published through Amazon saw things differently. They posted their own petition on Change.org—and gathered ten times as many signatures, more than 8,600. They appealed not to Amazon but to book buyers:

Without you [readers] there wouldn't be a book industry. We [self-publishers] owe you so much, and we are forever in your debt. . . .

New York Publishing once controlled the book industry. They decided which stories you were allowed to read. They decided which authors were allowed to publish. They charged high prices while withholding less expensive formats. They paid authors as little as possible. . . .

Amazon, in contrast, . . . allow[s] all writers to publish on their platform, and they pay authors. . . .

Rather than innovate and serve their customers, publishers have been resisting technology. They could have invented their own Internet bookstores, their own e-readers, their own self-publishing platforms. Instead, fearing the future, they fought to protect the status quo. . . .

Hachette is looking out for their own interests, not the interests of writers or readers. This approach is consistent with a long history of treating bookstores as customers, writers as chattel, and readers as non-entities. . . .

Don't let the wealthiest of writers convince you to turn away. . . .

Amazon didn't ask us to write this, or sign it. Amazon isn't aware that we're doing this. Because in the end, this isn't about Amazon. It's about you, the reader, and the changes you've helped bring about with your reading decisions.

Amazon surprised industry observers by stifling sales of *all* Hachette tittles, including the publisher's superstar, James Patterson. The year the controversy erupted, 2014, the *New York Times* reported that Patterson's name appeared on the cover of one of every seventeen books sold in the United States (6 percent). Why did Amazon toss all that income? Because the Amazon-Hachette conflict transcended mere revenue splits. It was actually a battle for the soul of the third book business, which depends on the long tail.

Patterson's sales were crucial to Hachette's bottom line. But not to Amazon's. Amazon cares less about selling huge numbers of the few blockbusters than about selling any numbers of everything else. While it's astonishing that any single author could account for 6 percent of all trade sales, Amazon made much more from the other 94 percent of sales—which is why the site could do what publishers considered un-thinkable: mess with Patterson.

During the conflict, Hachette's sales dropped 19 percent. Then Amazon announced a new contract with Simon & Schuster, and soon after, Hachette reportedly accepted similar (undisclosed) terms. The news media explained that Amazon granted Hachette more control over discounting, while Amazon won higher promotional fees, suggesting a win-win. But analysts declared Amazon the clear winner. Amazon got its promotional fees and earned more from them than Hachette gained from the changes in discounting.

About those mandatory promotional fees. Publishers consider them extortion. As one publisher told me, Amazon's mandatory fees are "a lot of money for doing nothing." Publishing savant Mike Shatzkin: "The overall direction of the book market continues to tilt toward Amazon."

Amazon: God's Gift to Self-Publishing Authors?

Self-publishing allowed authors to produce books, but could they sell them? Not through most bookstores. Few booksellers stock self-pub-lished titles. Booksellers already have more than enough books to sell, and instead of a modest number of professional reps hawking big lists, booksellers found themselves besieged by hordes of needy self-publishers each peddling a title or two, then pestering them daily about why their masterpieces hadn't sold. Fortunately for self-publishers, Amazon welcomed them with open arms.

Amazon graced self-published books with pages indistinguishable from the majors' titles. In addition, Amazon's Kindle Direct Publishing service (now Amazon Publishing) enabled cost-efficient publication of self-published books, both print and e-titles. Finally, when self-published work sold, Amazon paid its authors up to 70 percent of the gross.

Amazon proclaimed itself frustrated authors' salvation. When the media blared that a few self-published authors sold huge numbers and made fortunes, many self-publishers called Amazon a godsend.

Except for one little detail. Hardly any self-publishers struck it rich. The few who did almost invariably wrote romance novels or mysteries/thrillers. Other self-published authors' odds of selling more than a thousand copies are on the order of winning the lotto.

In addition, if self-published titles sell, authors may not collect the money due them. Search "book royalty fraud" and myriad accusations appear, accusing various self-publishing platforms of failing to credit authors for sales, pay contracted royalties, or even respond to emails.

Self-Publishing Success (Despite Amazon)

Soon after the Hachette contretemps, many successful self-publishers saw their Amazon incomes suddenly plummet—after Amazon introduced its Kindle Unlimited (KU) subscription service, free for the first month, then $11.99. Like its main subscription competitor, Scribd, KU offered instant access to millions of titles. But when subscribers obtain books through KU, their authors make much less than they previously earned from Kindle sales of their e-books. Some self-publishers saw their incomes drop 75 percent.

Kindle Unlimited looked like a raw deal not only for self-publishers but also for Amazon. Many devoted romance readers spent $100 a month on their favorite genre. But using KU, they could read all they wanted for just $11.99.

Why did Amazon launch a service that slashed its income? The Everything Store issued no comment, but analysts suggested that Amazon considered the service a loss leader. The site attracted readers with KU's low price, then surrounded Kindle text with ads for other Amazon products. But e-book authors have only one product to sell. If books are loss leaders, authors eat the loss.

Some authors opted out of KU. Others cut their books' prices to less than a dollar to compete with KU. Whatever happens going forward, Amazon appears to be something less than self-publishers' best friend.

Despite KU, the San Francisco author Josie Brown makes what she calls a decent living through Amazon sales of her darkly comic thriller series, Housewife Assassin. With a background in marketing and advertising, she published several commercial novels through major publishers but considered their marketing efforts lame. Brown pitched the majors on a thriller series about a soccer mom who moonlights for a shadowy government agency as a sexy assassin. They all declined. *Who's going to believe a housewife could be an assassin?* So Brown self-published her series through Amazon. She releases two Housewife Assassin e-books per year. Her series now includes more than twenty titles. Most sell for $2 to $5. She also prints through Ingram's Lightning service, so her books appear in the company's database. Her well-manufactured trade paperbacks can be ordered through any bookstore.

On the final page of each book, Brown encourages readers to join her email list. Over ten years, she's signed up seventeen thousand. When new releases hit, she emails her list and typically sells five thousand copies fairly quickly. With two dozen books in her series, her sales also enjoy a long tail. In addition, Brown markets her books through Barnes & Noble and Kobo, Canada's leading online bookseller. Finally, she organizes bookstore panels with multiple authors to have a shot at attracting crowds. Altogether, her series has sold well over a hundred thousand copies.

Note: This strategy may work for some mystery/thriller and romance fiction authors who release at least one book a year, build followings, and market relentlessly. It is far more difficult to do this with, say, biographies, historical fiction, or self-help titles—genres with less frequent releases and greater difficulty building followings. Not to mention that Josie Brown's strategy requires a tremendous amount of time and effort. She's both author and publisher, and at the prices she charges, her robust sales may result in only modest net earnings. Of course, she reaps the intangible rewards of commanding a large audience, and she can revel in the satisfaction of proving wrong the publishers who rejected her series.

The Unexpected Revival of Independent Booksellers

From 1995 to 2009, three-quarters of independent booksellers went bankrupt, and many of the rest looked moribund. But a funny thing happened on the way to the boneyard. Starting in 2010, against all expectations, new independent bookstores opened and thrived:

American Booksellers Association Membership

Year	Number of members
2009	1,401 (the low point)
2010	1,410 (the first increase in fifteen years)
2015	1,712
2019	1,887
2023	2,185 (with multiple locations, some 2,500 total stores)

The owners of several of these new bookstores were noted authors: Ann Patchett (in Nashville), Larry McMurtry (Archer City, Texas), Louise Erdrich (Minneapolis), Judy Blume (Key West, Florida), Jonathan Lethem (Blue Hill, Maine), and Jeff Kinney (Plainville, Massachusetts).

How do they survive Amazon? In the words of the Harvard Business School professor Ryan Raffaelli, by embracing the three Cs: community, curation, and convening. Successful indie booksellers have resurrected what many bookshops were during the first book business, community centers for readers and writers. They offer carefully curated titles and multiple ways for book lovers to meet and pursue passions for reading and writing.

One thriving indie is Book Passage in Corte Madera, California, just north of San Francisco. Book Passage hosts five hundred author events a year. It sponsors a dozen writing classes—everything from sentence construction to crafting novels. The store also presents language classes (Spanish, French, Italian, German, and Japanese) and kids' programs (games, puppet shows, reading groups). Book Passage organizes several annual weekend conferences focused on writing specialties: food, travel, mystery, children's, and literary fiction. Want to join a book group? The store sponsors dozens and discounts the titles its participants read. Or for a modest fee, readers can join book groups facilitated by well-read bibliophiles. Book Passage also features a café with an extensive menu and a collector's corner offering signed first editions, and it supports a speaker series at a local college—with staff selling presenters' books at the back of the room. Finally, the store promotes its myriad offerings through a newsletter emailed to thousands around the Bay Area.

Other bookstore–community centers sponsor board game contests, operatic voice recitals, open mic nights for singers and comedians, and birthday and engagement parties, all aimed at drawing crowds and making money, while also selling books.

Booksellers Go Toe to Toe Against Amazon on the Internet—Finally!

Indie booksellers are smart and entrepreneurial. As Amazon drove 75 percent of their sisters out of business, why didn't the American Booksellers Association or a coalition of indie booksellers launch an e-commerce site to compete directly against their hated foe?

I've asked many booksellers about this. They all knew they were looking into the wrong end of a cannon but said the ABA and its members lacked the capital, tech expertise, logistical support, and distribution capabilities to compete effectively against Amazon.

Back in the 1980s, years before Amazon, when the publishing innovator Jason Epstein learned of the then embryonic internet, he quickly envisioned harnessing it to sell books, especially backlist titles. At the time, books were not yet digital files. Publishers were releasing record numbers of titles, and warehouses were stuffed to overflowing. Publishers were forced to take an increasing proportion of books out of print, which pained Epstein. His idea? Use the new internet to market the hundreds of thousands of backlist titles in danger of disappearing.

He approached Prodigy, an early internet platform, about offering a huge catalogue of backlist titles. But Prodigy was interested only in new releases. Epstein shelved his idea. (Prodigy folded in 2001.)

A decade later, during the late 1990s when Amazon was still a puppy, Epstein realized it could become the big dog. In *Book Business*, he describes approaching publisher friends about developing their own Amazon:

"What I had in mind was a consortium open to all publishers, old and new, large and small, on equal terms. This consortium would create a combined annotated catalog of all its titles and maintain warehouses where books from diverse publishers would be packed and shipped directly to internet buyers." The major publishers weren't interested, and Epstein, who identified as an editor and publisher, did not approach the ABA.

In 2008, the ABA launched IndieBound.com, which developed reading lists and helped drive visitors to independent booksellers. But IndieBound didn't sell books, and the site was difficult to use, which is why few people outside of the book business have ever heard of it.

By 2011, publishers felt the noose tightening, and three majors—Penguin, Hachette, and Simon & Schuster—partnered on a joint book-selling website, Bookish, which launched in 2013 and quickly flopped.

Enter Andy Hunter. In 2018, the mid-forties entrepreneur ran a midsize New York literary publisher, Catapult, that also published a magazine and offered writing workshops. He loved the way indie book-sellers championed his literary titles. He also liked IndieBound—but thought it should sell books. He approached the ABA. The organization declined, saying it lacked the capital to transform IndieBound into a bookseller. But the organization said that if Hunter pursued his idea, the ABA might invest.

In 2020, with financing from angel investors and interest from two hundred booksellers, Hunter launched Bookshop.org, its mission to entice book buyers away from Amazon toward independent booksell-ers—just in time to help independent booksellers survive the COVID pandemic. Bookshop.org invited booksellers to set up pages where they could offer as many titles as they wished. When people click "Add to

Cart" and check out, the site processes orders, Ingram fulfills them, and the originating indie pockets 30 percent. ABA support helped Bookshop.org recruit stores. Today, participants include the large majority of indie booksellers in the United States and Canada and many in the UK.

Bookshop.org also sells audiobooks and e-books. The site claims sales of $40 million annually, about 1 percent of Amazon's gross from trade books, and has transferred $30 million to its indie bookstore partners. If you like the convenience of online book buying, but would rather support indies than enrich Amazon, visit Bookshop.org.

25

The Likely Future of the Book Business

The Great Merger Quashed

The third book business changed the reason for mergers. No longer were they last gasps before bankruptcy. In the twenty-first century, mergers became opportunities to expand backlists to capitalize on impulse book buying.

In 2020, Paramount announced its intention to sell Simon & Schuster. The house was quite profitable, but Paramount wanted to stream video, not sell books. S&S owned an enormous backlist. Bertelsmann, the German owner of Penguin Random House, offered $2.18 billion.

The merger would have combined the nation's two largest publishers and turned the Big One and Trailing Four into the Colossal One and Distantly Trailing Three.

Agents, authors, and the Authors Guild objected, saying the merger violated antitrust laws. Agents would have fewer houses to pitch, meaning fewer bidders for books, resulting in lower advances, especially for big-name authors. S&S and PRH countered that antitrust legislation targeted monopolies that hurt consumers by raising prices. But no publishing merger had ever raised book prices. Since the 1990s, in constant dollars, book prices had *fallen*. The proposed merger would not change that.

But the Supreme Court had previously ruled that mergers could be presumed illegal if the combined firm controlled at least 30 percent of any market. S&S-PRH would have controlled over 50 percent of trade book sales.

During the trial, the Justice Department presented antitrust experts who estimated that if the two houses merged, advances for top authors would fall by around $100,000 per title, with total advance reductions of $30 million annually. The two houses countered that only 7 percent of the majors' high-advance contracts involved competing bids from the two of them, an insignificant proportion. And even if the government correctly estimated advance reductions of $30 million a year, that figure represented only three-tenths of 1 percent of the $9-billion-a-year trade book market. In other words, the merger was insignificant.

The Justice Department called a celebrity witness, a top author for fifty years, Stephen King. He testified that since the 1970s when his first novel appeared, the number of publishers had steadily dwindled, and authors' advances had inexorably declined—not his, but the great majority of authors whose books were not bestsellers. He cited the 2022 Authors Guild survey showing that full-time authors' median annual income from book writing was only $12,000, and for part-time authors, the vast majority of AG members, just $2,800.

In 2022, a federal judge prohibited the merger. The ruling's wording suggested that going forward, none of the Big Five would be allowed to merge. That remains to be seen. But if future mergers are prohibited, none of the majors will be able to feather their nests by acquiring more huge, lucrative backlists.

According to Mike Shatzkin, the decision represented a "sea-change" in antitrust enforcement, "going from protecting consumers from high prices to protecting producers from low-ball bidding for the rights to publish their work." He added: "The five biggest publishers are probably at their high water mark for market share."

Shatzkin was prescient. Capitalism idolizes growth. If the Big Five can no longer increase their market share—that is, if they can't grow significantly—we would expect their value to fall. Simon & Schuster's value has fallen. Shortly after the PRH deal collapsed, the investment firm Kohlberg Kravis Roberts & Company purchased the house for $1.62 billion, a price $560 million (26 percent) less than PRH's offer.

Going Forward . . .

The future is unpredictable, and as social systems become more complex, their futures become even less foreseeable. Trade book publishing is a huge $9-billion-a-year enterprise, with many moving parts. To be sure, no one has a crystal ball, but today's book business is the product of six centuries of trends. An appreciation of those trends allows educated guesses about what the future might bring:

Expect bookstores to continue their transformation into community centers for readers and writers. I've heard booksellers complain that they went into the business to sell books, not coffee, croissants, and greeting cards. Sure, and I became a writer to pen the Great American Novel and spent four decades in the trenches of health journalism. Life's tough, and the third book business is sending booksellers a clear message: If you want to sell books, you better sell more than just books. Booksellers need to sell experiences, destinations. Around the country, the most successful bookstores do this. The message to authors is also clear: If you want booksellers to embrace your work, embrace them back. The next time you buy a book on the internet, consider the world you want to live in and choose your bookseller carefully.

Options for author camaraderie should continue to grow. Using the internet, it's easier than ever for authors to establish online platforms and find ways to make friends, both virtual and in real life. Authors have plenty of opportunities for interaction: conferences, workshops, bookstore panels, MFA programs, regional organizations (e.g., Maine Writers and Publishers Alliance), national organizations (the Authors Guild, the National Writers Union, the Association of Writers and Writing Programs), and more book festivals, author residency programs, summer writing camps, and writer-oriented websites than ever. They all invite authors to meet, critique one another's work, share their joys and frustrations, and ponder the promise and challenges of the third book business. However, authors reap in community only what they sow in participation. One stereotype is that authors are recluses holed up in little rooms typing. Yes, writing is a solitary pursuit, but to make the most of the process and the results, I've found it really helpful to hang out with other authors, notably at gatherings convened by the Authors Guild. And within the community of authors, don't forget indie bookstores. They help generate word of mouth, the single best way to sell books.

The Big Five should do fine, at least for a while. Compared with the numbers from the 1990s, sales of most new titles have dwindled. But digital publishing has cut publishers' costs somewhat, and bestsellers and large backlists have kept them in the black . . . so far.

The Big Five's corporate overlords are not sentimental. If they saw trouble ahead, they would unload their publishing properties. So far, they haven't. Yes, Paramount sold Simon & Schuster, but not because it was failing. Shortly after the court derailed S&S's proposed merger with

Penguin Random House, S&S reported *increased* sales and income. The majors appear to be doing fine. But Amazon looms, and if there's one key truth in the third book business, it's this: publishers need Amazon much more than Amazon needs them.

Amazon is likely to gain increasing leverage over publishers. Jeff Bezos launched Amazon as a bookstore well before it sold anything else—and used books so successfully as bait to sell other items that in publishing, the term "loss leader" has become an expletive. Today, on Amazon's balance sheet, book sales are a mere footnote. Amazon grosses $525 billion a year, trade publishing $9 billion. Approximately 40 percent of publishers' incomes flow through Amazon, some $3.6 billion. That's less than 1 percent of Amazon's gross. The Everything Store could stop selling books tomorrow and hardly notice. But if publishers suddenly lost $3.6 billion in sales, they'd be devastated—until other booksellers filled in. But that might come too late.

The public has largely forgotten Amazon's 2014 dustup with Hachette, but publishers have not. On the surface, things appear to have returned to normal. But *l'affaire* Hachette strikes me as a shot across the bow, Amazon telling publishers, *Don't mess with us.* While I have no inside information, it looks like Amazon decided to back off from confrontation and play a longer game. In other words, Amazon has dropped the frog into the pot and is raising the temperature slowly, at every inflection point squeezing more money out of publishers, which over time weakens them.

Not long ago, the major publishers controlled genre fiction. Today, Amazon Publishing accounts for a big chunk of those sales, which hits publishers where it hurts. Amazon might also fatten up at publishers' expense in other ways:

• As contracts expire, Amazon will almost certainly demand more favorable terms and larger promotional fees.

• Amazon Publishing might expand into children's books, juvenile titles, cookbooks, travel, or other lucrative niches, seizing more of publishers' market share.

• And with the collapse of the merger of Penguin Random House and Simon & Schuster, it becomes much harder for the majors to grow their backlists. This weakens publishers and, over time, strengthens Amazon.

Mike Shatzkin notes, "If big houses can't grow organically [i.e., from new releases], there are very few smaller houses [with significant backlists] to acquire, and anti-trust prevents them from combining with each other, they are doomed to a long, slow decline."

Over time, the frog appears to be on its way to getting cooked. If that happens, the conglomerates might eventually decide to sell. To whom? How about Amazon? In 2013, when Jeff Bezos purchased the then struggling *Washington Post*, he said he was delighted to preserve the media icon. Since his acquisition, the *Post* has done okay. Bezos might say the same about buying moribund publishers. *The conglomerates were ready to kill them. I saved them!* Then over time, Amazon Publishing might quietly turn the majors into imprints and control the book business. Who knows?

Ingram might flex its muscles. Ingram (since 2009 Ingram Content Group) does not have a monopoly on trade book distribution. Baker & Taylor distributes to thousands of libraries, and Amazon distributes books released by its publishing arm. But Ingram boasts a database of an estimated twenty million titles and a huge print-on-demand operation for both publishers and self-publishing authors.

What if Ingram suddenly raised its fees for book distribution and print-on-demand? Until a viable competitor emerged, publishers and self-publishers would have to pay up. Could a competitor beat Ingram on price and service? Possibly eventually, but probably not for quite a while. If Ingram raised prices, publishers and self-publishers would certainly suffer, then probably stick with Ingram and accept smaller slices of the pie. In the foreseeable future, what alternative would they have?

Control of the third book business looks like a battle between Amazon and Ingram. The first book business was author-centric; the second, publisher-centric. The third looks increasingly sales-and-distribution-centric.

Book publishing involves manufacturing, promotion, distribution, and sales. In 1999, publishers manufactured and promoted books, and Ingram and Amazon distributed and sold them. But in the twenty-first century, any schnook can manufacture quality books in all formats quickly and cheaply, and Amazon and Ingram can promote and sell them as well as publishers, if not better. Consequently, publishers' hundred-year-old business model looks increasingly threatened.

The distribution game has three major players: Amazon, Ingram, and Baker & Taylor. B&T is by far the smallest, therefore appealing for acquisition by one of the other two. Which leaves Amazon and Ingram. Amazon has long enjoyed the higher profile. But quiet, behind-the-scenes Ingram looks equally well positioned to dominate the third book business.

Both companies control the digital files for millions of books—Amazon much of genre fiction, Ingram pretty much everything else. Amazon is a superefficient store, but it doesn't control the books it sells. Amazon might remedy that by buying one or more of the Big Five and snatching their digital files from Ingram. Ingram might also buy one or more of the Big Five.

What Ingram lacks is a bookstore. But the company does business with Bookshop.org. As I write, Bookshop.org is a mere sapling to Amazon's mighty oak. But imagine Ingram acquiring a controlling interest in Bookshop.org and building it out sufficiently to compete with Amazon. Ingram would likely increase its market share at Amazon's expense—Godzilla vs. King Kong.

The conglomerates haven't sold any major publishers . . . yet. But publishers no longer reign over the book business, and going forward, they look increasingly vulnerable—and ripe for acquisition by Amazon or Ingram. Billions of dollars are at stake, and both Amazon and Ingram can be expected to fight tooth and nail to grab the brass ring. Whichever company does, the third book business appears headed for domination by distributors. What would this mean for publishers, authors, booksellers, and agents? That's not clear, but as the book business becomes more sales-and-distribution-centric, incomes for everyone else look increasingly threatened.

Authors' incomes should continue to fall. The Authors Guild surveyed more than five thousand members about their writing incomes in 2009, 2015, and 2022. During those thirteen years, authors' incomes dropped by *half*. What's happening to authors mirrors what's happened to musicians and actors. Musicians used to make modest royalties from LPs and CDs. Actors used to make "residuals," royalty payments when their TV shows or movies were syndicated. Streaming services have upended that. They pay considerably less.

Now, more than ever, writers must understand the business they're in, starting with a realistic definition of "success." Fame and fortune have become much less likely, so what else is there? Personal satisfaction? Leaving a legacy? Participation in a community of writers? Authors need to answer that question for themselves.

For all but the biggest names, advances appear likely to decline or disappear as no-advance contracts become the rule. As of 2024, we're a quarter century into the third book business. Publishers continue to pay the big names huge advances, with several thousand other authors a year offered at least some money up front. But with two million new releases every year, only a fraction of authors now receive advances. I got no advance for this book and feel fine about it. I'm a writer. I felt passionate about writing this book. Advance or no, I feel delighted that you're holding it in your hands. And if you bought it, I make a little money.

Royalties appear headed from "gross" to "net." Some publishers have quietly shifted the basis for royalty payments from books' cover price, "gross income," to publishers' "net revenue," that is, what's left after bookseller discounts, Amazon fees, and other expenses. Contracts that specify royalties based on "net revenue," aka "net sales proceeds," cut publishers' royalty obligations. If you're offered a book contract, read it carefully. Your royalty rate may well be lower than you think. If you have questions, ask the Authors Guild.

These days, many contracts have jettisoned the twentieth-century practice of specifying different royalty rates for different formats, instead substituting one rate for all editions. The contract my agent negotiated for this book offered 30 percent of net revenues, around 10 to 12 percent of the gross. I felt okay about that. I was raring to write this book, and like 99.99 percent of authors, for me, book writing has always been a sideline. Meanwhile, my publisher is trying to eke out a living in a very dangerous game. He has no house in the Hamptons. I'm at peace with our arrangement.

Agents appear increasingly threatened. Advances are down. Sales are increasingly iffy. And authors' incomes have plummeted. How can agents live on 15 percent of less and less? A survey by the Association of American Literary Agents shows that in 2023 almost one-third of agents made less than $50,000 a year. Incomes are especially low for young agents just starting out. They typically apprentice with established agencies for several years and make little more than the minimum wage. According to the survey: "The pay structure is cited as the main contributor to the burnout felt by younger agents, leaving some respondents to wonder if agenting offers a viable professional path." Many young agents have side gigs: freelance writing or retail or food-service jobs. Some mid-career agents have moved to a hybrid model, collecting 15 percent if books sell to majors but, if not, charging authors set fees for sales to indie presses or publishing books through their own PSCs.

On the Authors Guild community forum, some writers have declared they would never pay agents a dime before books sell. That's shortsighted. How are agents supposed to survive in a world of shrinking advances? Their 15 percent was not handed down from Sinai. They charged 10 percent well into the 1980s. Then mergers began reducing the number of publishers agents could pitch. Surviving publishers ratcheted down their offers. To cope, agents raised their fee to 15 percent.

Now the third book business has disrupted things again. Personally, I would have no problem paying an agent an up-front fee, with the money refunded if 15 percent of any advance topped that amount.

Publishing appears headed for a hybrid model. Since the millennium, the avalanche of self-published books has cratered sales of most new releases. The Big Five can pay the bills with backlist sales, but most small- and medium-size publishers lack huge backlists and don't have that luxury. How can they stay afloat? By returning to the model of the late nineteenth and early twentieth centuries: paying to publish books they believe have strong sales potential, while charging everyone else to publish.

If you're an author with an agent, pitch the Big Five first. If one offers an advance, take it. If not, you have three choices: (1) accept a no-advance deal, (2) pay a publisher or PSC to release your book, or (3) self-publish.

Over eighteen years, three drafts of this book struck out with the Big Five. I rethought my approach one more time and wrote a fourth draft, and my agent pitched it. I was delighted to sign a no-advance contract with Unnamed Press. The deal has several upsides:

• You're reading *The Untold Story of Books*.

• No advance means no indenture to pay off. I've made money from the first copy sold. If you bought this book, my deepest thanks.

• And no advance means Unnamed is more likely to stay in business.

As far as I'm concerned, that's a win-win. Of course, other authors must make their own decisions.

Expect many editors to launch PSCs. Publishers aren't the only book people founding PSCs. Book editors are also doing it. Most editors are overworked and underpaid. Some have gone off on their own by launching PSCs that emphasize editing. Editorial polish makes books shine and resonate with readers, reviewers, and tastemakers. Comparing PSCs that just publish (Kindle Direct and others) with PSCs that offer all levels of editing (developmental, line, and copy, plus proofreading and fact-checking), I would choose the latter.

Artificial (stolen) intelligence. As this book goes to press, tremendous controversy surrounds generative artificial intelligence (AI), the growing ability of computers to generate nuanced written material that appears to have been written by humans. Like all previous technological innovations, AI has unleashed blue-sky predictions of huge social benefits and dystopian visions of mass layoffs of white-collar workers. Only time will tell. But one thing is crystal clear. AI companies have ripped off authors. AI gained its vaunted intelligence through book piracy.

Generative artificial intelligence originates in "large language models" (LLMs), huge libraries of text that AI developers use to train computer systems to mimic human writing. Where did AI developers obtain the mountains of text their machines crunched into LLMs? They stole it from authors whose copyrights they ignored. For many AI developers, the LLM of choice is BookCorpus, a huge dataset compiled in 2014 by researchers at MIT and the University of Toronto. BookCorpus has helped train several LLMs, including OpenAI's GPT and Google's BERT.

The developers of BookCorpus mined the Smashwords platform, assimilating 7,185 e-books that contained seventy-four million sentences. Smashwords' terms of service specify that the e-books it publishes may be read but not plagiarized, resold, or reused in any way. The Book-Corpus site says its LLM was developed using "unpublished" e-books. Wrong. The e-books BookCorpus cannibalized were published and are the intellectual property of their authors, who never licensed their use and received nothing. BookCorpus pirated their work. Consequently, generative AI developers—and users—benefit from larceny.

Another LLM creator, Prosecraft, used book-pirating websites to cannibalize twenty-seven thousand books without permission. After protests from authors and the Authors Guild and threats of lawsuits, Prosecraft shut down. Yet another AI book pirate is Meta. The Facebook parent's Books3 database gobbled up 180,000 books—including three of mine and eleven titles released by this book's publisher. (Authors who want to learn if Books3 has stolen their work should contact the Authors Guild.)

Of course, AI book piracy comes as no surprise. The internet has devalued all information. The book business was founded on piracy. And the digital revolution has made it easier than ever. The Authors Guild and other advocates for creators have demanded compensation for text used in AI training. As this book goes to press, several lawsuits have been filed, including one by the Authors Guild and many prominent authors, including John Grisham, Jodi Picoult, Jonathan Franzen, and George R. R. Martin. But I'm not holding my breath waiting for checks from the AI thieves.

AI threatens all creators: authors, screenwriters, visual artists, copywriters, editors, illustrators, and on and on. AI was a key issue in the Hollywood strikes of 2023, and going forward, we can expect more contention over control of creative endeavors. Some call it a fight for the soul of humanity. Stay tuned.

Long-form reading is resilient. Nothing can kill books. This is the first of two predictions I'm absolutely sure of. As technology evolves, new innovations are bound to seize the public imagination and prompt renewed predictions of books' demise. But repeatedly, new technologies have *not* killed book reading. Nothing ever has, and all evidence suggests nothing ever will. Not everyone spends their leisure time reading books, but a huge swath of the population *loves* to read and won't stop, no matter what new widgets software engineers dream up.

Authors will continue to write. Here's my other certainty: six centuries of little or no leverage haven't dissuaded authors from searching for the perfect word. Human beings are creative. Countless millions love to write. We writers yearn to express ourselves in words, and to do that, we're willing to make sacrifices. After fifty years in the writing game, I have many scars but few regrets. I wake up every morning eager to stare at the blinking cursor and wrestle with words. Yes, the book business is bittersweet. It always has been and looks like it always will be. But for me, the joy of writing books and seeing them published and read compensates for everything else.

No one can predict the future. But life unfolds like a good book. We keep turning pages to see what happens next.

═ Acknowledgments ═

During the eighteen years I spent intermittently working on this book, a small army of friends, authors, professional editors, and publishing people read various drafts and provided wise and sometimes blunt counsel.

Highest praise goes to the best editor I've ever worked with, my brother Deke Castleman, an ace at all levels of editing.

Deepest thanks to my agent since 2002, Amy Rennert of the Amy Rennert Agency, Tiburon, California. During the years I worked on this book, I produced three drafts that Amy worked hard to sell, but no publisher bought. When I mentioned I was working on draft number four, a lesser agent might have declined representation, saying the book was unsalable. But Amy liked my revised approach and beat the bushes. She even came up with the title. Deepest thanks, Amy.

Many thanks to Chris Heiser, publisher of Unnamed Press, for sensing value in an economic history of book publishing. Thanks also to Nancy Tan, my copyeditor, and the team at Unnamed Press, Allison Miriam Smith, Jaya Nicely, and Cassidy Kuhle.

Appreciation to the late Paul Aiken, former executive director of the Authors Guild, who granted me access to the Authors Guild *Bulletin* archive.

Thanks to Andrew Kovacs at R. R. Bowker, who supplied year-by-year information about ISBNs.

Many thanks to my agents from 1978 to 2002, John Brockman and Katinka Matson of Brockman Inc., New York, who sold ten of my books.

Perpetual thanks to the editors and friends who critiqued the four drafts: Belle Adler, Randy Alfred, Daniel Ben-Horin, Mary Claire Blakeman, John Boe, Josie Brown, Jean Burgess, Chris Carlsson, Jeff Castleman, Maya Castleman, Mim Castleman, Steve Castleman, Virginia Castleman, Mark Chimsky, Dennis Church, Frank Colin, Nancy Dunn, Alice Feinstein, Charles Fracchia, Joan Frank, Laura Fraser, Jeff Gillenkirk, Joe Goldenson, Larry Gonick, Sam Guckenheimer, David Hankin, Laird Harrison, Mark Hertsgaard, Pat Holt, Dan Hubig, Gina Hyams, Beth Kephart, Jeffrey Klein, Marty Klein, Katherine Kocel, Eddie Krasnow, Clyde Leland, Laura Lent, Fred Levine, Ron Lichty, Virginia London, Marc Mauer, Elissa Miller, David Neuman, Eve Pell, Stan Pesick, Charles Piller, Carla Ruff, Phil Ryan, Mike Shatzkin, Anne Simons, Jane Sloven, Larry Smith, David Steinberg, Jim Steinberg, Peter Straus, Trisha Thompson, Frank Viviano, Tony White, and Robin Wolaner.

Finally, my deepest thanks and boundless love to my wife, Anne, who rarely reads nonfiction but critiqued several drafts of this book.

═══ Sources and Bibliography ═══

This book involved forty years of research. Sources include: the Authors Guild *Bulletin*, the Authors Guild community forum, Authors Guild Bay Area chapter meetings, Publishing Professionals Network meetings, a dozen writers conferences, several publishing conferences and book festivals, the *New York Times*, the *New Yorker*, the *Wall Street Journal*, *Publishers Weekly*, *Publishers Lunch*, *The Shatzkin Files*, WordsRated, Book Industry Study Group reports, Statista reports, Bookreporter, articles in many other periodicals, and these books:

Anderson, Chris. *The Long Tail: Why the Future of Business Is Selling Less of More*. New York: Hachette, 2014.

Appelbaum, Judith. *How to Get Happily Published*. 5th ed. New York: Harper-Perennial, 1998.

Bailey, Herbert S., Jr. *The Art and Science of Book Publishing*. 1970. Athens: Ohio University Press, 1990.

Biel, Joe. *A People's Guide to Publishing: Build a Successful, Sustainable, Meaningful Book Business from the Ground Up*. Portland, OR: Microcosm Publishing, 2018.

Bodian, Nat. *The Joy of Publishing: Fascinating Facts, Anecdotes, Curiosities, and Historic Origins about Books and Authors, Editors and Publishers, Bookmaking and Bookselling*. Fairfield, IA: Open Horizons, 1996.

Bowerman, Peter. *The Well-Fed Writer: Financial Self-Sufficiency as a Commercial Freelancer in Six Months or Less*. 3rd ed. Atlanta, GA: Fanove Publishing, 2021.

Cerf, Bennett. *At Random: The Reminiscences of Bennett Cerf*. New York: Random House, 1977.

Duncan, Dennis. *Index, A History of the: A Bookish Adventure from Medieval Manuscripts to the Digital Age*. New York: W. W. Norton, 2023.

Eckstut, Arielle, and David Henry Sterry. *The Essential Guide to Getting Your Book Published: How to Write It, Sell It, and Market It . . . Successfully!* New York: Workman, 2010.

Eisenstein, Elizabeth L. *The Printing Press as an Agent of Change: Communications and Cultural Transformations in Early-Modern Europe*. 1979. Cambridge: Cambridge University Press, 2009.

Epstein, Jason. *Book Business: Publishing Past, Present, and Future.* New York: W. W. Norton, 2002.

Friedman, Jane. *The Business of Being a Writer*. Chicago: University of Chicago Press, 2018.

Gaughran, David. *Let's Get Digital: How to Self-Publish and Why You Should*. 4th ed. Self-published, DavidGaughran.com, 2020.

Ginna, Peter. *What Editors Do: The Art, Craft, and Business of Book Editing*. Chicago: University of Chicago Press, 2017.

Gomez, Jeff. *Print Is Dead: Books in Our Digital Age*. New York: Palgrave Macmillan, 2008.

Gottlieb, Robert. *Avid Reader: A Life*. New York: Farrar, Straus & Giroux, 2016.

Greco, Albert N., Clara E. Rodríguez, and Robert M. Wharton. *The Culture and Commerce of Publishing in the 21st Century*. Stanford, CA: Stanford University Press, 2007.

Greco, Albert N., Jim Milliot, and Robert M. Wharton. *The Book Publishing Industry*. 3rd ed. New York: Routledge, 2014.

Grimes, Martha. *Foul Matter*. New York: New American Library, 2004.

Hall, Frania. *The Business of Digital Publishing: An Introduction to the Digital Book and Journal Industries*. London: Routledge/Taylor & Francis, 2013.

Houston, Keith. *The Book: A Cover-to-Cover Exploration of the Most Powerful Object of Our Time*. New York: W. W. Norton, 2016.

Howard, Nicole. *The Book: The Life Story of a Technology*. Baltimore, MD: Johns Hopkins University Press, 2009.

Isaacson, Walter. *Ben Franklin: An American Life*. New York: Simon & Schuster, 2004.

Kachka, Boris. *Hothouse: The Art of Survival and the Survival of Art at America's Most Celebrated Publishing House, Farrar, Straus & Giroux*. New York: Simon & Schuster, 2013.

Kaestle, Carl F., et al. *Literacy in the United States: Readers and Reading since 1880*. New Haven, CT: Yale University Press, 1991.

Kawasaki, Guy, and Shawn Welch. *APE: Author-Publisher-Entrepreneur—How to Publish a Book*. Self-published, Nononina Press, 2013.

Korda, Michael. *Another Life: A Memoir of Other People*. New York: Random House, 1999.

Lamott, Anne. *Bird by Bird: Some Instructions on Writing and Life*. New York: Anchor Books, 1995.

Lukeman, Noah. *The First Five Pages: A Writer's Guide to Staying Out of the Rejection Pile*. New York: Simon & Schuster, 2000.

McGurl, Mark. *Everything and Less: The Novel in the Age of Amazon*. London: Verso, 2021.

Menaker, Daniel. *My Mistake: A Memoir*. Boston: Houghton Mifflin Harcourt, 2013.

Miller, Laura J. *Reluctant Capitalists: Bookselling and the Culture of Consumption*. Chicago: University of Chicago Press, 2007.

Nissenbaum, Stephen. *The Battle for Christmas: A Cultural History of America's Most Cherished Holiday*. New York: Vintage, 1996.

O'Donnell, David G. *The Old Corner Book Store: The Story of Ticknor and Fields*. Cambridge, MA: Pocket Metro, 2010.

Perkins, Maxwell E. *Editor to Author: The Letters of Maxwell E. Perkins*. Edited by John Hall Wheelock. New York: Scribner, 1950.

Phillips, Angus. *Turning the Page: The Evolution of the Book*. London: Routledge, 2014.

Price, Leah. *What We Talk about When We Talk about Books: The History and Future of Reading*. New York: Basic Books, 2019.

Rabiner, Susan, and Alfred Fortunato. *Thinking Like Your Editor: How to Write Great Serious Nonfiction—and Get It Published*. New York: W. W. Norton, 2003.

Rein, Jody, with Michael Larsen. *How to Write a Book Proposal: The Insider's Step-by-Step Guide to Proposals that Get You Published*. 5th ed. Cincinnati, OH: Writer's Digest Books, 2017.

Schiffrin, André. *The Business of Books: How International Conglomerates Took Over Publishing and Changed the Way We Read*. London: Verso, 2000.

———. *Words & Money*. London: Verso, 2010.

Shatzkin, Leonard. *In Cold Type: Overcoming the Book Crisis*. Boston: Houghton Mifflin, 1982.

Shatzkin, Mike, and Robert Paris Riger. *The Book Business: What Everyone Needs to Know*. New York: Oxford University Press, 2019.

Sinykin, Dan. *Big Fiction: How Conglomeration Changed the Publishing Industry and American Literature*. New York: Columbia University Press, 2023.

Striphas, Ted. *The Late Age of Print: Everyday Book Culture from Consumerism to Control*. New York: Columbia University Press, 2009.

Tager, James, and Clarisse Rosaz Shariyf. *Reading between the Lines: Race, Equity, and Book Publishing*. PEN America, 2022, https://pen.org/wp-content/uploads/2023/01/Reading-Between-the-Lines.pdf.

Tebbel, John. *A History of Book Publishing in the United States*. 4 vols. New York: R. R. Bowker, 1972–1981. Reprint, Harwich Port, MA: Clock & Rose Press, 2003.

Thompson, John B. *Book Wars: The Digital Revolution in Publishing*. Cambridge, UK: Polity Press, 2021.

———. *Merchants of Culture: The Publishing Business in the Twenty-First Century*. Cambridge, UK: Polity Press, 2011.

Whiteside, Thomas. *The Blockbuster Complex: Conglomerates, Show Business, and Book Publishing*. Middletown, CT: Wesleyan University Press, 1981.

Woll, Thomas. *Publishing for Profit: Successful Bottom-Line Management for Book Publishers*. 5th ed. Chicago: Chicago Review Press, 2014.

=== Index ===

Michael Castleman grew up in Lynbrook, New York, a Long Island suburb of New York City. He graduated Phi Beta Kappa from the University of Michigan with a degree in English and earned a masters in journalism from the University of California, Berkeley. An award-winning journalist, he specializes in health and sexuality and was twice nominated for National Magazine Awards. Over the past fifty years, he has written three thousand magazine and web articles, fifteen nonfiction books, and four mystery novels. His bimonthly blog on Psychology-Today.com, *All About Sex*, has amassed more than sixty million views. He lives in San Francisco. Castleman welcomes comments on *The Untold Story of Books*. Visit mcastleman.com.